INTERLINK ILLUSTRATED HISTORIES

Anti-Semitism

T0017508

Other titles in the series

Castro and Cuba by Angelo Trento

Gandhi and India by Gianni Sofri

Hitler and Nazism by Enzo Collotti

Middle East Conflicts by François Massoulié

Mussolini and Fascism by Marco Palla

The Spanish Civil War by Gabriele Ranzato

INTERLINK ILLUSTRATED HISTORIES

ANTI-SEMITISM

FROM ITS EUROPEAN ROOTS TO THE HOLOCAUST

ROBERTO FINZI

Translated by Maud Jackson

INTERLINK BOOKS

An imprint of Interlink Publishing Group, Inc.

New York

Chapter 1

THE **E**NEMY **W**ITHIN

AFTER CENTURIES OF HARSH DISCRIMINATION, THE JEWS OF WESTERN EUROPE GAIN EQUAL RIGHTS UNDER THE LAW. BUT IN THIS MATERIALISTIC AGE, ANTI-SEMITIC PROPAGANDA IS STILL ALIVE AND WELL, SUSTAINING AN IRRATIONAL DEMONIZATION OF THE JEWISH PRESENCE IN MIDDLE-CLASS SOCIETY.

In 1983 a book entitled *L'affaire*, by Jean-Denis Bredin, was published in Paris. The French public had no need of further details: despite the passage of almost a century, for them "the Affair" could only mean the Dreyfus case, on which subject Bredin's work is still the best.

At the time, the Dreyfus affair had an extraordinary impact on public life. Take, for example, the comments in *Avanti*, an Italian socialist daily (22 August 1899):

> These days the Dreyfus affair is the most important and conspicuous fact in contemporary international politics; newspapers in all countries ... dedicate their columns and pages to the developments of that dramatic trial.

The trial in question was conducted before a court martial in Rennes, and lasted from August to September of 1899. Alfred Dreyfus, a Jewish captain of artillery in the French army, was accused of treason.

The story began in the summer of 1894, when the Italian anarchist Sante Caserio assassinated the French President Marie François Sadi Carnot at Lyons. Caserio, who was finally guillotined, shot Carnot because the French head of state had not given amnesty to Emile Henry, another anarchist. After the assassination of their president, the National Assembly passed exceptional laws against anarchists, known as the "wicked laws". These events exacerbated a

*L*eft: group photograph of a family of Spanish Jews in Rhodes at the beginning of the century. They were the descendants of the Sephardic community that was forced to leave Spain in 1492.

Below: a 1628 print of the Jewish ghetto in Frankfurt am Main. The long semicircular street that cuts across the picture from top left to bottom right is Judengasse *(Jew Street), which marked one of the limits of the ghetto.*

climate in which there was already a strong and growing nationalist tendency.

Maurice Agulhon wrote:

Nationalism is opposed to anything that threatens "to fragment the nation or change its nature, or, sooner or later, to justify other nations in criticizing it". At best, therefore, nationalism defines itself not so much by hostility to other nations, however common that feeling might be among nationalists, as by hostility to *the enemy within*, the anti-national, the international, the supranational. And it was precisely in the nineties that the enemy within took the form of the Jew, or rather the myth of the Jew.

Why should the Jew be seen as "the enemy within"? Who were the French Jews, and what did they do, to give shape to this idea? To understand what was happening in France at the end of the nineteenth century, and the enormous significance of the Dreyfus case, it is first necessary to take a few steps backwards.

Only the newly-independent United States of America had preceded France in considering the Jews to be

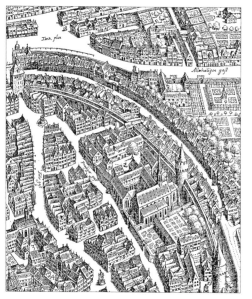

citizens like all others. In Europe it was the "great revolution" of 1789 that gave them fully equal rights. French Jews as a whole were finally liberated from the legal restrictions that had characterized their state since medieval times in September 1791; only the slaves had to wait longer (they were emancipated in 1794). And it is significant that the same word was used to describe the attainment of equal rights for Jews and for slaves: emancipation.

But the Jewish community's new-found equality under the law had little effect on ancient and deeply-rooted prejudices; nor could it be otherwise. These prejudices were continually reinforced by the liturgy, by religious teaching and practice that nourished and kept alive a popular and scholarly tradition that permeated the collective consciousness: the spectre of the Christ-killing Jew.

That spectre is at the root of a myth that flourished in Europe from medieval times to well past the beginning of the twentieth century: the ritual homicide of Passover. According to this sinister myth, at Passover Jews kill a Christian child, whose blood is then spread on the unleavened bread of the Passover feast.

When Popular Imagination Alters History

The Christ-killing of which the Jews have stood accused for centuries is not merely a distant and abstract theological idea. It is a story endlessly repeated from childhood onwards, supplemented by an infinite number of sacred images which refer to it directly or indirectly. It is the story, above all, of a betrayal — a betrayal for money. The message it transmits is very clear: the Jew is greedy and treacherous; he conspires behind the backs of his benefactors. Isn't this the Judas Iscariot of popular imagination? The complex theological meaning of the Christian story is lost in a collective perception that is best exemplified in the changed meaning of the word "Judas": once a proper name, it has become a synonym for "traitor". This Judas image — a corruption of a religious figure — "explains" the real nature of the Jew for the anti-Semite. Don't "Judases" dedicate themselves to rapacious professions that exploit the poor and needy? Aren't many usurers Jews?

Here the popular imagination — and prejudice hardened in the popular imagination — transcends history entirely. All historical sources attest that through the centuries Jews followed a variety of professions, often lowly. One such testimony is to be found in the work of Bernardino Ramazzini, the standard-bearer of the workers' health-care movement. In his discussion of workers' illnesses, *De morbis artificum diatriba* (1700), he describes Italian Jewish communities (especially those located in Rome) as made up for the most part of people who worked in humble capacities, such as rag-and-bone men, mattress-

This fourteenth-century picture shows the distinguishing sign that identified a Jew.

THE CHURCH AND THE JEWS

At the end of the eleventh century, the time of the Crusades to the Holy Land, the geography of the hereafter was changed forever with the insertion of a "third world": purgatory. The Church at that time condemned usury, but purgatory meant that even the (Christian) merchant, who aside from buying and selling also lent money at interest, had the possibility of reaching eternal salvation.

But the merchant was not only a usurer: he was also a money-changer and a banker, functions necessary to his legitimate, viable profession of commerce, whose profits were the result of work.

The preaching of the Crusades had serious consequences for European Jews. Pope Urban II proposed the liberation of the Holy Land in 1095 at the Council of Clermont-Ferrand. To the cry "It is God's will", knights, monks and people of low rank left their homes and families. They sewed the symbol of the Cross on their clothes: they were God's avengers, born to punish all infidels. A chronicler of the period described the various infidels as "Jews, heretics and Saracens". The year 1096 was studded with massacres of Jews. On the road to the Holy Land the crusaders "cleansed" the Christian realms, ridding them of "infidels". The principal actors in these anti-Jewish excesses were for the most part crowds of poor people who, following the armies, abandoned themselves to violence against the Jews. This is evidence of widespread anti-Jewish sentiment.

The historian Léon Poliakov observed that after the preaching of the Crusades, "every time medieval Europe was dragged along by a great religious movement, every time that Christians faced the unknown for the love of God, hatred against the Jews increased a little everywhere". The Jew, always in a precarious position because he was subject to the possibility of persecution and expulsion, was thus forced by his circumstances to seek the protection of kings and obtain "privileges" — papers that per-

mitted him to live somewhere in safety. He was given this protection in exchange for money. For the Jew, therefore, money was not simply a means of obtaining his daily bread or becoming rich: it was as necessary to him as air; he needed money to live in safety, to avoid being hunted down, to flee from persecution. Besides its own commercial requirements (economic reality necessitated the practice of lending of money with interest), Christian society's tolerance of "usury" among the Jews (regulated and controlled by civil and religious authorities) was also connected to the special status

of the Jew in Christian theology. The death of Christ — theologians remind us — was a necessary sacrifice because it opened the way to redemption for all humanity. Those who caused it were thus instruments of the divine plan; in this way they proved the truth of what was foretold in the Holy Scriptures. The Jew was thus living evidence of the realization of biblical prophesy; and he must continue to exist in order to perform this function. In theory, then, the Jew's right to life and all that follows from it was assured. At the same time, however, the Jew must be punished as one of those responsible for the Crucifixion. In the words of the celebrated Catholic preacher Vincenzo Ferrer (1350–1419), "Christians should kill the Jews not with the knife but with the word". The image of the knife was commonplace; the word was used continuously, not only in preaching but also in laws that separated Jews from the Christian population (segregating them in ghettos), forbade them to own buildings or land, placed impediments in the way of their social advancement, and relegated them to marginal professions of dubious legality in which their "greed" was always — of necessity — evident. ■

makers, shoemakers, and repairers of old clothes.

A similar account describes the French Jews of Alsace, which was annexed to the German Empire after the French defeat of 1870. At the time of emancipation, this province was home to the largest population of French Jews, "people from all the nations of Europe who came laden with children and rags". Laws, customs and statutes forbade them to own land or enjoy the benefits of the community, and excluded them from many professions. Thus French Jews were reduced to living as travelling merchants, buying rags and used clothes and selling them at a small profit. The most fortunate were dealers in horses, livestock or feed. Alternatively, they were moneylenders. And here again we come face to face with the greedy Jew whose "earthly god" is money, as the young Karl Marx (well known to have come from Jewish stock himself) wrote in 1843.

Left: a Jewish text of the fifteenth century, which describes the conventions of the Passover ritual. Below: Crusaders and Saracens confront each other in battle; the scene is taken from the Chronicles of Alfonso X of Castile *(fourteenth century).*

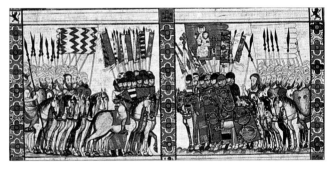

Moneylending was one of the few professions legally permitted to Jews in medieval Europe. Based on a much debated interpretation of two passages from the Bible (Deuteronomy 23:20, "unto thy brother thou shalt not lend upon usury"; and Luke 6:35, "lend, hoping for nothing again"), the Church had severely condemned lending money with interest. In the deliberations of the Lateran Council of 1139, for example, it was said that those who practise it "must be considered infamous throughout their lives, and, if they do not repent, they must be denied a Christian burial". Thus the significance of the word "usury" changed radically: originally a technical word meaning the price to be paid for the *use* of borrowed money, over the centuries it assumed a purely negative sense (excessive or illegal interest charged on a loan). The condemnation of the Church was the turning-point in this mutation of meaning. And because of its negative connotations,

*A*bove: *Jews, accused of sacrilegious rites, are burned alive in this fifteenth-century German print.*
Right: a print portraying the sacking of Jewish homes in Judengasse, Frankfurt, in 1614.

from the Middle Ages on there was a continuous search for euphemisms so that the word "usury" could be avoided.

Once more, history shows the inaccuracies of the stereotype. If "usurers" are people who lend money, then they can be found in all commercial societies — ancient, medieval and modern. It follows that there is nothing specifically Jewish about lending money with interest. Certainly, in many parts of medieval Europe, some of the Jewish community were moneylenders. But why? They were in fact obliged to follow that profession by external pressure, and not as the consequence of any "natural" tendency in Jews themselves, as anti-Semitic interpretations would have us believe.

If more evidence were needed of the groundlessness of these anti-Semitic claims (which are repeated *ad nauseam* even today), we could consider another historical fact that is too often ignored. Like any minority, the Jews have had a tendency to endogamy (to marry among themselves). Anti-Semites therefore assert that *they have always been the same*, from ancient times to the present: that they transmit their perverse genetic heritage unadulterated from generation to generation.

As ever, the anti-Semite is not concerned with how often this has actually occurred. The Jews haven't always been self-sufficient, so to speak, in their demographic growth: in Hellenic times, in Roman times, and up to the eleventh century, Judaism showed a great capacity to attract converts from the population among whom its adherents settled. Medieval Jews, pushed towards usury by the pressure of the "external" world of the majority, were, like every people, the result of many different genetic inheritances, many different "natures". And did their culture or faith predispose them to lend money with interest? Not in the least.

After all, the passage from Deuteronomy that was used to justify the Christian condemnation of usury is a Hebrew text, and even the New Testament is a product of Jewish culture.

Does Emancipation Erase Discrimination?

The Dreyfus case exploded at the end of 1894. A few years earlier, France had celebrated the centenary of the 1789 Revolution, which among other things had emancipated the Jews. After emancipation some French Jews moved toward assimilation: they gradually abandoned their distinctive costume, married Gentiles, and sometimes even converted to Christianity. The majority of those who were assimilated had never been practising Jews, and learned the lessons of liberalism quicker and more readily than other sectors of the Jewish population. The great and essential liberal idea of tolerance for every faith implied that, in time, religious differences would diminish, and that the minority would be assimilated into the majority.

Many remained Jewish, seeing emancipation as a way to overcome the discrimination that had oppressed them for centuries and become at last an integral part of the society in which they lived; they refused to be assimilated, but directed all their efforts towards becoming integrated instead. There is evidence of this in the kinds of work they did. Anyone — whether Jewish or not — who wondered whether emancipation was necessary could see that the occupational and social situation of the Jews was anomalous, because of the discrimination to which they had been subjected. Above all, there were few "producers", especially agricultural producers. It was expected that emancipation would make the social composition of the Jewish population similar to that of other populations. But what actually happened was that the

Those who refused to be assimilated directed all their efforts at becoming integrated instead.

JEWS AND USURY

Jewish tradition embraces various attitudes towards usury, of which three are particularly important. The *Talmud*, the essential reference book of the Jewish religion, permits but does not recommend the lending of money with interest. Authoritative Talmudic scholars taught that one of the ways of reaching perfection was to lend without asking for interest, not only to one's brothers but even to the "gentiles". Perfection — or, to use a different language, sainthood — is, however, a condition to which few can aspire and which very few attain. But the idea that lending without interest is the behaviour of someone who tends towards perfection necessarily presupposes that normal behaviour is different: it implies that the moneylender has a right to interest.

In the Byzantine Near East a second train of thought developed among Jewish theologians, according to which "the profit derived from usury, even if the borrower is an idolater, is bound to lead to ruin". By contrast, the great Jewish thinker Moses Maimonides (1135–1204) maintained that to require interest of a non-Jewish borrower is a *commandment*. These last two positions, diametrically opposed to each other, have their origins in the same desire: to defend the purity of the Mosaic religion. Those who condemned absolutely the lending of money with interest, even if the borrowers were non-Jews, were anxious to prevent two things from happening: they didn't want the Jews to "follow in the footsteps of the

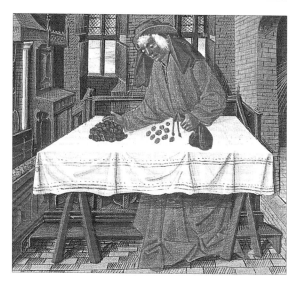

gentiles" (who are thus implicitly accused of being greedy and corrupt in their monetary dealings); and they didn't want Jewish moneylenders to pass gradually from a clientele of gentiles to a clientele of their fellow-Jews. Those, like Maimonides, who held that it was right — that it was even a duty — to exact interest on a loan to a "gentile", thought that the Faith was at less risk of being compromised if the relations between Jews and "infidels" were limited to business. A loan without interest could sow the seeds of friendship, a much more intense relationship which might induce doubts or even conversions among the Jewish minority living in that great Christian ocean. In the Middle Ages and thereafter, up to "emancipation", only a part of the Jewish community was employed in moneylending.

And there were enormous differences among these "usurers", who ranged from small lenders to great financiers. The Rothschilds, the world-famous bankers so often evoked by modern anti-Semites, far from representing the Jewish community as a whole do not even represent the majority of Jewish moneylenders.

Even in the Middle Ages, as in the modern and contemporary world, Jews pursued different professions. Many bought and sold used clothes. At first this was an occupation freely chosen from among the few that were open to Jews. In some places it later became the only occupation open to them, as in the Papal States, where from the late sixteenth century Jews had to limit themselves to the rag trade by order of the Papal government. ■

majority of Jews diversified their occupations within the commercial sector, abandoning their itinerant jobs to open small shops and businesses. In an era of capitalist expansion, they used their long experience of the market economy for their own social advancement. And it was precisely because of this upward social mobility that French Jews were never completely assimilated into the surrounding gentile society.

Citizens with Equal Rights

The persistence of certain cultural differences is a sign of integration: the French Jews felt they were part of a society in which they could be themselves and at the same time be recognized as citizens with equal rights. Gradually the Jews diversified their occupations. They joined the liberal professions; they went into politics, public administration, and the armed forces. An apposite example of this last was Captain Alfred Dreyfus, son of a rich mercantile family, who chose to serve in the army.

Is the enthusiasm that French Jews felt for their country, the first nation in Europe to concede full citizenship to Jews, also evidence of the disappearance of anti-Semitic prejudice in French society? Perhaps the best reply to that question can be found in a letter by the German Jewish writer Ludwig Börne (originally Loew Baruch). In Paris in January 1832 he wrote: "Some reprove me for being a Jew, others praise me for it, still others pardon me for it, but everybody thinks about it." The emancipated Jew did not cease to be a problem; in fact, his new status as a citizen with equal rights brought about a backlash of anti-Semitism.

There was still a strong current of traditional Catholic anti-Jewish sentiment in nineteenth-century France. There were explosions of anti-Semitic violence, as for example in Alsace in 1848. The first intimations of modern racism also appeared around this time. Joseph-Arthur de Gobineau's four-volume discussion of the

Left: a fifteenth-century usurer counting money in his shop. Below: this late-nineteenth-century photograph shows a shoemaker of Romanian origin with his family outside their shop in Paris.

Below: Captain Alfred Dreyfus in a 1906 photograph, at the end of the tortuous political-juridical process in which he was the protagonist. The Dreyfus affair was one of the most striking cases of anti-Semitism.
Top right: the Catholic writer Edouard Drumont, ensign of the French anti-Dreyfus campaign and author of the best-selling book Jewish France.
Bottom right: the French philosopher Pierre-Joseph Proudhon, one of the best-known exponents of so-called "economic" anti-Semitism.

inequality of the races — *Essai sur l'inégalité des races humaines* (1853–5) — had an especially strong influence in Germany. Gobineau was not in fact anti-Semitic: he considered the Jews "a free people, a strong people, an intelligent people, who have … given the world almost as many scientists as merchants." Nevertheless, Gobineau is remembered not for his favourable judgment of the Jews but rather for his idea that humanity is divided into different "races", arranged in a hierarchy so that some are superior to others.

In France a new form of contempt for Jews was gaining ground: so-called "economic" anti-Semitism. This was disseminated mainly by intellectuals of left-wing and socialist tendencies, who saw the Jews as the beneficiaries of the social injustices of bourgeois society. The works of some of the best-known French socialist theorists give us glimpses of harsh anti-Semitism. For Pierre-Joseph Proudhon (1809–65) — perhaps the first to refer to the Jews as "the race of Sem" — "the Jew has an anti-productive temperament: he is neither farmer nor industrialist nor even really entrepreneur. He is an intermediary, always fraudulent and parasitic." None of the works of Charles Fourier (1772–1837) is complete without its attack on the Jews. His anti-Jewish ideas were systematized by one of his disciples, Alphonse Toussenel, who in the mid-1840s published a volume entitled *Les Juifs, Rois de l'Époque* (*The Jews, Kings of the Epoch*). Even the early works of Marx echo the phrases of economic anti-Semitism.

Why Did Anti-Semitism Become Popular?
Despite all this, up until the early 1890s anti-Semitism in France had little political importance. At the end of 1882, *Le Figaro* observed: "An anti-Semitic movement such as that which is gaining ground in various parts of the globe would, in France, immediately become the object of popular ridicule." Marcel Proust testified that in the same period the Catholic bourgeoisie warmly welcomed the Jews. Only with the Dreyfus affair "all that was Jewish, even an elegant lady, slid down, and obscure nationalists climbed up to take their places."

From the mid-1880s onwards the situation changed. The clearest sign of this new reality was the success of Edouard Drumont's book *La France Juive* (*Jewish France*, 1886). Drumont was a Catholic and a Republican. *La France Juive* (1,200 pages in two volumes, with an index of over 3,000 entries) is full of anecdote and scandal: combining Christian anti-Jewish sentiment with occultism, racism and economic anti-Semitism, it represents history as an apparently interminable struggle between Jews and non-Jews. In one year alone, it was reprinted 114 times and sold 150,000 copies.

The success of *La France Juive* is evidence that, in contrast to what *Le Figaro* had asserted a few years earlier, by 1886 entire social classes had adopted an attitude of irrational demonization towards the Jewish presence in France (which actually amounted to only 70,000 to 80,000 people, no more than 0.2 per cent of the population of the Republic). Why did anti-Semitism become so popular in those particular years? The answer contains several elements, but first let us consider the economic crisis.

Between 1882 and 1890 France was in the grip of a long recession: fear and a sense of insecurity spread through the population. At the beginning of this period the Union Générale — a Catholic bank founded with the express purpose of combating the supremacy of Protestant and Jewish families in the field of finance — suffered a spectacular collapse. The Union's principal clients were ecclesiastical bodies, rich Catholic families, and thousands upon thousands of

Traditionally, the Jew is an infidel who has refused the Word of the Redeemer. At any moment he could, by converting, become a member of God's Church.

ordinary parishioners with modest savings accounts. In 1882 management errors caused the bank to fail, but obliging journalists with links to the clerical world attributed the failure to the secret manoeuvres of groups of Jewish financiers, led by those "Jews *par excellence*", the Rothschild banking family. The debate was lengthy and had widespread ramifications. It mattered little that the main proponent of the theory of Jewish machinations against the Catholic bank was its director — one of those responsible for the Union's management errors, and also a former employee of the Rothschilds.

The Perverse Logic of the Conspiracy

In 1892 another financial scandal affected many people's savings: the failure of the Panama Canal Company, founded by Ferdinand de Lesseps, the architect of the Suez Canal. He had nothing to do with Judaism; nonetheless, Jews were once again held responsible for the failure. Some Jewish financiers were involved in the scandal, but the "Jewish" character of the fraud was so entirely imaginary that, in its attempts to defend Lesseps at the beginning of the affair, the Catholic journal *Le Croix* paradoxically reversed the anti-Semitic argument. According to the reasoning of *Le Croix*, Jewish financiers were not the promoters of the great financial swindle that had robbed so many people of their savings, but rather the opposite: "Panama is left to die because it tried to act without submitting itself to the protection of Jewish financiers." As always, it was the fault of the Jews ...

In *La France Juive*, Drumont wrote, "Today the Semites believe themselves to be secure of victory. It is no longer the Carthaginian or the Saracen who leads the movement, but the Jew; he has replaced violence with shrewdness... Instead of attacking Europe head on, [the Jews] have crept up behind her; they have tricked her." Drumont had no doubts: the weapons of the Jew had been the Revolution and the principles of 1789. "The only one to have profited from the Revolution is the Jew." And the result? "After eighteen centuries," Drumont claims, "nothing has changed ... I see only one image … the image of Christ insulted." Was this a renewed expression of Christian — and in particular Catholic — anti-Jewish sentiment? There is no doubt that the stereotype of the treacherous Christ-killing Jew was rooted in the collective imagination. It was certainly part of Drumont's cultural baggage, and he used it to the utmost.

At the end of the nineteenth century this archetype was enhanced by the darker shades of modernity. Traditionally, the Jew was an infidel who had refused the Word of the Redeemer. At any time he could, by converting, become a member of God's Church. But, in the age of positivism and materialistic values, hostility to Jews took on different characteristics: the Jew was now marked by the stigma of "race". In 1902 a French philosopher, a materialist with theoretical and nationalist political tendencies, observed: "The fertilized ovum

Surrounded by his worshippers, the golden calf looms large on the cover of the French daily Le Petit Journal. *In 1892, at the height of the uproar over Panama,* Le Petit Journal *blamed Jewish financiers for the collapse of the Panama Canal Company, giving expression to the latent prejudice that condemned the Jews and their supposed idolatry.*

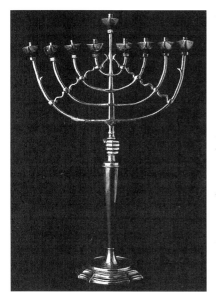

of an Aryan or of a Semite necessarily reproduces the biological characteristics of the race or of the species, body and soul, just as happens with … any other mammal." He continues, "If a Jewish child is raised from birth in an Aryan family … neither nationality nor language will modify by one atom the genetic make-up of that Jew." It is not difficult to see, in this as in other racist texts, the unjustified leap from biological heredity and transmission to psychological characteristics; to sustain such a thesis one must rely on absolute scientific falsehoods.

Economic anti-Semitism added another dimension to the hatred of the Jews, halfway between social indictment and racism. For Toussenel, the Jew was a symbolic figure. "Like the people," he wrote, "I call by this name — despised Jew — every trafficker in money, every unproductive parasite who lives off the substance of the work of others. Jew, usurer, trafficker: for me these are synonyms." The Jew here is a metaphor. But this metaphor (the practical effects of which have been devastating) represents every single Jew as the bearer of those characteristics,

JESUITS PREACH APARTHEID AGAINST JEWS

The passage that follows is taken from the first 1898 issue of Catholic Civilization, *a Jesuit magazine founded in 1850. Its point of departure is the Dreyfus case; from there it develops into yet another call — as in the times of the ghettos — to separate Jews from the society in which they lived.*

In France (and consequently elsewhere), anti-Semitism is now found less in its economic form and ever more directly in its political form. And it meets with general agreement, as is already evident in the various proposals of legal restrictions which are now under discussion everywhere and, for the first time, deemed necessary by the majority. For the Jew, racial *solidarity* is prior to and above any feeling of patriotism. This has been proven beyond question by the Dreyfus case. The Jew, naturalized though he may be, never ceases to be first and foremost a Jew; only afterwards is he a citizen of the country in which he was born and which has given him equal rights with other citizens. Today this is seen as an incontrovertible truth. It is therefore now up to the French to make sure that the pretence of judicial error, fabricated in 1897 by Jews in order to save one of their number who is a traitor to France, gives way to a clear demonstration of the real political error committed by the assembly that gave French citizenship to the Jews in 1791. That was the starting point of all other freedoms, the results of which the nation is suffering so bitterly today. ■

no matter what his true character might be. And this is no accident: "The god of the Jewish people is none other … than Satan… The religion of the Jewish people has made them irrevocably the enemies of humanity". Thus economic anti-Semitism combined with religious anti-Jewish sentiment and gained strength from it.

Why does the Jewish religion turn its adherents into the "enemies of humanity"? The victim of the so-called Christ-killers — argued the militants of nascent socialism — was Christ, and Christ, betrayed by the ecclesiastical hierarchies, was the first socialist: he who proclaimed the moral pre-eminence of the "last". Thus anti-Semitism became tinged with a "leftist" aura. But between the radical left and the right lay the criticism of democracy which in its turn was combined with the attack on the Jews.

Naturally, the right and the radical left attacked democracy from opposing points of view, but sometimes their attacks converged. Both concluded that political democracy was a deception: behind the apparent "power of the people" was a political elite motivated by personal interests and representing hidden powers. All this seemed to confirm the conspiracy theory.

For those who adopted the conspiracy theory, the Jew became a privileged subject. Who could be more inclined to conspiracy than those who descended from the same stock as Judas Iscariot, a man capable of plotting behind the back of the Redeemer himself? If you think about it, who are the real holders of power in contemporary society? Those who have a great deal of capital. Isn't great finance "Jewish"? And don't Jews live in all countries, making them, by definition, non-national? Would it be surprising to learn that "international capital", as embodied in the Rothschilds, was in cahoots with the "international revolution" that sought to demolish the state and change the nature of the nation? France itself, argued the anti-Semites, could show unimpeachable evidence of the "Jewish plot": the foundation in Paris in

Left: a brass Hanukkah lamp, which is lit during the Jewish festival in memory of the inauguration of the Temple in Jerusalem. Above: an 1885 print portraying Nathaniel Rothschild, a member of the English branch of the great banking dynasty. The Rothschild family originally came from Germany.

This late-nineteenth-century print portrays a couple from the Hassidic Jewish community of Eastern Europe.
Right: a French cartoon of the banker Rothschild extending his sinister influence over the world.

1860 of the Alliance Israélite Universelle (Universal Israelite Alliance) by a group of prominent Jews.

Two Serious Incidents Stir Public Opinion

The Alliance was a defensive reflex, founded in response to the celebrated Mortara case and the emotion it stirred all over Europe.

The case began in Bologna in 1858. One morning, in this second city of the Papal States and the seat of the oldest university in Europe, papal troops burst into the home of a Jewish family called Mortara and seized their little son, Edgardo. The father tried to mobilize the press and foreign public opinion. Napoleon III and Franz Josef, both Catholic monarchs, advised Pope Pius IX to restore the child to his family. The pontiff replied with two terrible words: *Non possumus* (we cannot).

Why had the child been torn from his parents? Why did the Vatican not succumb to pressure, even from two such important monarchs? The Mortaras of Bologna had a Christian housemaid. When Edgardo was one year old, this housemaid had baptized him in secret; some time later she told her confessor about the secret baptism. Without delay, they set in motion legal mechanisms which permitted the ecclesiastical authorities to separate a baptized child from his non-Christian parents by force.

Shortly after the abduction of Edgardo, Bologna ceased to be part of the Papal States. The father then tried again to get his son back. Edgardo, in the meantime, had been taken to a religious institution in Rome. All that international pressure managed to achieve was the concession that when he reached his majority Edgardo Mortara would be permitted to see his father and choose which religion to follow. The boy was educated in Catholicism so that he might be ordained a priest. At twenty-one years of age, he "freely" chose Catholicism. He became a priest, and eventually an eminent prelate of the Roman Curia.

Eighteen years earlier another famous anti-Jewish incident had rocked Europe: the Damascus affair. In February 1840, in Damascus, Syria (which was then under Ottoman rule), a Franciscan monk and his server mysteriously disappeared. Rumour had it that the last place the monk had been seen was the Jewish quarter; it was only a short step from this to saying that the Jews had killed him. The French consul was influenced by these rumours and believed them to be true, as did the Ottoman authorities.

Why should the Jews have killed the monk? According to the testimony of a Jewish butcher, who in the course of two interrogations had been given a total of 350 lashes on the soles of his feet, it was to get Christian blood to spread upon their unleavened bread at Passover. According to the confession, the order had been given by the rabbis. Arrested by the police, the accused denied the charges and were tortured. In the end the prisoners confessed, having endured days of sleep deprivation (guards, working shifts night and day, stopped them from sleeping). Ritual homicide was therefore "proved" against the Jews of Damascus, and those responsible were condemned to death. The Sultan annulled the verdict because of pressure from European governments, urged on by European Jews and especially some of their leaders, such as Moses Montefiore (1784–1885), an active defender of Jewish identity

Between a certain sector of the radical left and the right there was another angle of agreement, which in its turn combined with the attack on the Jews: a refusal to grant them full democratic rights.

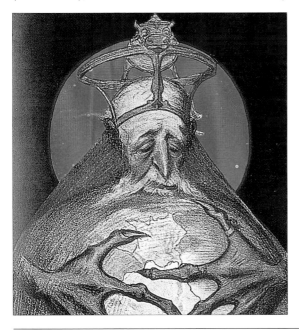

A calender of 1831, issued in Thessalonica. Each page gives the date in Arabic, French, Greek and Cyrillic, reflecting the variety of peoples who lived in the Greek city at that time. Right: a decree, issued the same year, regarding the economic rights of the Jews of Modena.

and rights. When the presumed murderers of Damascus were condemned to death, a delegation of European Jews went to Mehmet Alì, Viceroy of Egypt, under whose jurisdiction Damascus then lay. Montefiore led the delegation, and one of its members was Adolphe Crémieux, an important figure in the Jewish community and on the nineteenth-century French political scene.

In 1863 Crémieux became the President of the Alliance Israélite Universelle. The job was a difficult one. When the Alliance was founded in 1860, the emancipation of the Jews was still a long way off in many countries. Jews were not considered citizens or subjects with equal rights in what remained of the Papal States, the Iberian peninsula, part of Germany, the Hapsburg Empire, the Ottoman Empire, Russia, Switzerland or Sweden. Even in Great Britain the Jews didn't have full equal rights until 1871, although many rights had been won earlier.

For the Alliance, defending the Jews where their rights had been trampled upon meant not only fighting against cases of obvious injustice or persecution: it meant above all inculcating Western ideals in the hearts of the most withdrawn Jewish communities. But this exposed these communities to a possible double accusation: in the countries in which Jews did not yet enjoy recognized rights, such as Tsarist Russia, they were accused of colluding with those who wished to destroy the established government; in areas under pressure from European imperialism, like the Near East, they were accused of being in the pay of European imperial powers.

For the anti-Semites, the existence of the Alliance was proof that there really was a supranational Jewish organization which used emancipation to act in its own interests. The Jews were in cahoots with all the intriguers of Europe, and didn't give a damn about the good of the nation. The real enemy, they maintained, was the Jew, who used finance to exploit the people and impose his own power upon them. Economic crises, the failure of banks, anarchist uprisings — all proved this beyond the shadow of a doubt.

THE DICTATOR

OF THE CITY AND PROVINCE OF MODENA

—————◆—————

Decrees and orders as follows:

1. The law that prohibits Jews from owning or acquiring as property any kind of real estate outside the Ghetto is hereby repealed.

2. The provision of the law that prohibits Jews from managing rental properties outside the Ghetto is repealed; and thus the all the provisions from Article 16, Title 9 to Book 3 of the Legal Code, and all other provisions that obstruct the rights which are restored to the Jews by the present Law, are hereby repealed and abolished.

3. In consequence, the Jews will hereafter enjoy the right to possess and acquire real estate of any kind, whether it be inside or outside the Ghetto, and the right to make rental contracts and manage properties outside the Ghetto, as they will have the right to make contracts of exchange for properties.

4. In cases in which Jews have accepted real estate in adjudication, and still possess it, or the quinquennium has not yet lapsed at the end of which they would have to transfer it, they can retain such real estate and possess it, the provision of law that constrained them to transfer it within five years being hereby repealed. The present Law has the following restriction:

Jews cannot acquire, exchange or rent *houses and buildings outside the Ghetto, where the Ghetto exists, without a licence from the Government* that is valid at the time that the contract is undertaken; this is for reasons and motives that the present Provisional Government is convinced are for the public good of all citizens whatsoever.

The present Law will be printed, published and circulated throughout the Province of Modena, and the competent Authorities are authorized to execute it.

From the Residence of the Dictatorship this day 20 February 1831

NARDI.

—————◆—————

MODENA from the printing press of the Provisional Government

Chapter 2

THE DREYFUS AFFAIR

IN 1894 THE DREYFUS CASE EXPLODED IN FRANCE. UNJUSTLY ACCUSED OF ESPIONAGE, A JEWISH CAPTAIN IN THE FRENCH ARMY HAD TO WAIT TWENTY YEARS BEFORE HIS INNOCENCE WAS RECOGNIZED: A SAGA THAT BECAME SYMBOLIC OF THE STRUGGLE BETWEEN FREE THOUGHT AND PREJUDICE.

And so to the Dreyfus affair. In 1894, Hubert-Joseph Henry was an officer in the French Secret Service (he later became its director). At the end of September he received a piece of paper, torn in four, that had been found in the wastepaper basket of the German military attaché in Paris. It had been sent to him by a cleaning woman who was in the pay of the French Secret Service.

Justice is done: Captain Dreyfus leaves the École Militaire in July 1906, after having been reinstated in the ranks of the army.

That scrap of paper, which became known as the *bordereau*, contained notes written by a French officer who was clearly offering military secrets to the Germans. The investigators focused their attention upon Alfred Dreyfus, an artillery captain on the General Staff. It was later said that there was evidence against him, but that was not true: if there was any evidence at all, it had been fabricated after the fact.

The Odyssey of the Jewish Captain

Alfred Dreyfus had several characteristics that made him a suspect *par excellence*. He was from the artillery, and the information that the author of the *bordereau* had offered to the Germans was about the artillery. He was an officer on the General Staff, and the secrets in question would only have been available to officers of his rank. Dreyfus, however, had a peculiarity that distinguished him from all his fellow officers at army headquarters: he was a Jew. He wasn't the only Jew in the French army — far from it. There were many Jews among the French military cadres. But did this signify

On 4 June 1908, Dreyfus was the target of an assassination attempt. The moment was intensely symbolic: the Captain was attending a ceremony to commemorate the removal of Emile Zola's ashes to the Pantheon.

that the Jews were integrated into French society — or, in an anti-Semitic reading, that the tentacles of the "Jewish octopus" were insinuating themselves into the very vitals of the nation? In any case, Dreyfus was the only Jew on the General Staff.

On 14 October the Minister for War, General Auguste Mercier, ordered the arrest of Dreyfus. Although the evidence against him was flimsy, the trial went ahead without any guarantee of the rights of the accused. On 22 December 1894 Dreyfus was found guilty, and condemned to be stripped of his military rank and imprisoned for an unspecified time. On 5 January 1895 Dreyfus was taken to the penitentiary on Devil's Island.

From the beginning, the well-to-do Dreyfus family —

and especially his brother Mathieu — fought to prove Alfred's innocence. Some people were willing to listen, but the military hierarchy presented a impenetrable wall of deliberate deafness. The situation changed when, on 1 July 1895, Colonel Georges Picquart was appointed head of the information service of the French army. Re-examined by Picquart — who was Alsatian, like Dreyfus — the documentation of the trial revealed someone else who might have been guilty of the crime: Commandant Marie-Charles-Ferdinand Walsin Esterhazy. In March of the following year, Picquart had proof of Esterhazy's guilt: the handwriting of the *bordereau* was his, not that of Dreyfus.

At the beginning of November the campaign for a new trial was launched, with the publication in Brussels of *Une erreur judiciaire: la verité sur l'affaire Dreyfus* (*A Judicial Error: The Truth About the Dreyfus Affair*), by Bernard Lazare. This was the real start of the *affaire*, and the beginning of a long, hard battle. It didn't matter that, having left France on 11 November 1897, the German military attaché to whom Dreyfus was alleged to have sold military secrets declared, "I have never met Dreyfus." He confirmed this in his memoirs, which appeared in 1930, adding that Esterhazy was on the German payroll from July 1894 to May 1896.

During the long years of the *affaire* a central role was played by the novelist Emile Zola. By the end of 1897 he

Below: the poster in which the Paris business community declared its position on the Dreyfus affair. It reads: "Down with the Jews! Down with the traitors!" These are identified as Captain Dreyfus and the writer Emile Zola, who had defended the captain's innocence.

had already taken on the defence of Dreyfus. Then in early January 1898, Zola published his famous open letter to M. Felix Faure, the President of the Republic, better-known as "*J'accuse*" (I accuse) — in Clemenceau's newspaper *L'Aurore*. In this rigorously-argued letter, Zola denounced the judicial error and emphasized the complicity that had made such an error possible and had protected those really responsible for it.

The opposition camp represented Zola's position as an attack on the fundamental institutions of the state. Zola and *L'Aurore* were judged and condemned. In July 1898 Zola, having been found guilty of defamation of

the State, fled to England to avoid prison. At the end of August, Henry confessed that he had falsified documents which had been fundamental in the case against Dreyfus; he then committed suicide. The anti-Dreyfus camp made a hero of him, a victim of the obscure intrigues of the Jews. In early September Esterhazy fled, and in June 1899 he admitted that the *bordereau* — the document upon which the accusation against Dreyfus had been based — was written by him. He claimed, however, to have acted on instructions that were known to both the Minister for War and the head of the General Staff.

By this time the fabric of the accusations had crumbled; nevertheless, in the second trial of Alfred Dreyfus, conducted in August and September 1899 before a court martial at Rennes, the accused was convicted once more. Although extenuating circumstances were recognized, he was condemned to ten years' imprisonment. Ten days after the verdict of Rennes, Dreyfus accepted an amnesty from the government; but the battle to clear his name was not yet over.

In May 1902 the radical-socialist left was victorious

in the elections and the new Premier of France was George Clemenceau, whose newspaper had been the vehicle for Emile Zola's campaign on behalf of Dreyfus. The case was reopened, and an inquiry was set in motion. Zola died on 29 September 1902, but the *affaire* dragged on until 12 July 1906, when the Supreme Court annulled the sentence of Rennes. Dreyfus was reinstated as an army captain and Picquart also returned to the army, after having been the object of innumerable persecutions himself. On 25 October 1906, soon after the victory of the pro-Dreyfus camp was sealed, Clemenceau appointed Picquart Minister for War. Despite all this, however, the *affaire* continued to poison the political climate.

Two cartoons of the period: one shows a high official stirring up the affair, here represented as a sinister brew; the other shows Zola in the act of launching his attack against the highest ranks of the armed forces.

On 4 June 1908 Dreyfus was the target of an assassination attempt. The moment was intensely symbolic:

the captain was attending a ceremony to commemorate the removal of Emile Zola's ashes to the Pantheon.

A Battlefield Between Right and Left

Thus the *affaire* lasted for years and a great deal of time went by before the truth emerged, because by then the issue was not simply the fate of Captain Dreyfus. He had become the symbol of a dispute in which the foundations of the Republic were in question, a battlefield between the right and the left. In the end the pro-Dreyfus camp won, but they were a minority, an *avant-garde*, perhaps even an elite, before their view spread to the entire left wing in France.

The difficulties of supporting the Dreyfus cause were multiplied by the fact that the victim was a Jew. As Zola observed in *J'accuse*, Dreyfus was a "victim... of the persecution of 'dirty Jews' that dishonours our epoch". Zola did not light upon the phrase "our epoch" by accident. The *affaire* was not an isolated incident: it was part of a greater wave of anti-Semitism that flooded the whole of Central and Western Europe and often still had at its core the accusation of ritual homicide of Christians by Jews. The Dreyfus case, however, had specific characteristics that made it the *affaire par excellence*. It happened in France, birthplace of the concept of emancipation, where in the 1890s, the most virulent French anti-Semites discovered that suspicion of and resentment against the Jews could nevertheless find wide public consensus.

But did the *affaire* ever really come to an end? In 1985 a proposal to place a statue of the captain at the *École Militaire* created a deep controversy, resulting in the decision to place it in the Tuileries Gardens instead. Another example of latent anti-Semitism came to light on 31 January 1994, the centenary of the beginning of the *affaire*. A magazine published a note from the army's historical branch in which the innocence of Dreyfus

The front page of Le Petit Journal, *13 January 1895, showing the ceremony in which Captain Dreyfus was stripped of his rank and his sword was broken.*

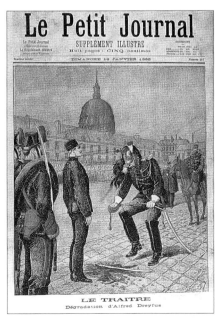

Le Petit Journal

SUPPLÉMENT ILLUSTRÉ

LE TRAITRE
Dégradation d'Alfred Dreyfus

was represented as nothing more than the version of events commonly accepted by historians… Only in 1995 did the French army declare officially that Dreyfus was innocent.

Even a century later the phrase "*L'affaire*" continues to function as a euphemism, because, according to the writer V. Duclert, "it embodied a certain kind of modernity" in that it obliged the nation to ask itself fundamental questions about the nature of citizenship, the Republic and the state. Intellectuals of both left and right — who found in the conflicts surrounding the Dreyfus case

"THE CURSE OF THAT RACE"

Edouard Drumont, a Catholic writer and leader of the anti-Semitic movement in France, gave expression to many popular prejudices in his 1894 polemic "*L'espionnage juif*" (Jewish Espionage). The cadence of the following passage is almost that of a sacred text, as if it were a decalogue designed to illuminate a single truth: that the Jew is by nature a traitor. Note how he extrapolates a general rule from a few specifics (each of which is in its way peculiar) — a thoroughly erroneous logic.

The case of Captain Dreyfus, which has provoked such strong emotions both at home and abroad, is nothing but an episode in Jewish history. Judas sold the God of Mercy and Love. Deutz betrayed the heroic woman who had trusted him. Simon Mayer tore the tricolore from the column of Vendôme and threw it in the dirt. Naquet and Arthur Meyer brought poor General Boulanger to his ruin. Meyer, the administrative official, helped the Jew Hemardinger to make faulty

instruments. Jewish butchers make our soldiers eat rotten meat. Captain Dreyfus sold the mobilization plans and the names of agents in the information service to Germany. It is the fatal destiny of the type and the curse of that race.

Analyzing the instances to which Drumont refers reveals the fallacy of this argument. The most famous, certainly the one that took deepest root in French popular imagination, was that of Simon Deutz. In 1832 he handed Maria Caroline of Bourbon-Napoli, Duchess of Berry, over to the government of Louis Philippe. In 1816 the Duchess had married Charles Ferdinand Bourbon, after whose death by assassination in 1820 she gave birth to a posthumous son, Henry, Duke of Chambord. In 1830, after the July Revolution, Henry became a pretender to the French throne. The Duchess of Berry defended her son's right against Louis Philippe, who had become King of France after the July Revolution. She made a vain attempt to topple Louis Philippe by means of an

armed revolt in Vandea, a region which had historically supported a legitimist tradition. Having failed in this attempt, the Duchess turned to Deutz for help, but he betrayed her. Deutz was a Jew who had converted to Catholicism. Therefore, according to Léon Poliakov, even if "the Holy Seat recommended this adventurer to the Duchess… the reproof went to the synagogue". In January 1898, when the Dreyfus case was at its zenith, the authoritative Jesuit periodical *Catholic Civilization*, adopted Drumont's approach and claimed that, when Dreyfus's "treachery" was discovered, "the nation brooded upon the record of the citizen-Jew, and remembered that Iscariot was of the same stock… Looking back at history, it found examples of Jewish treachery against the nation and the individual. The list of these examples — both in ancient times and more recently — was long enough." Thus traditional Catholic anti-Jewish sentiment converged with modern anti-Semitism, which speaks of "race". ∎

the occasion and stimulus for a new level of commitment — were the protagonists, so to speak, and also intermediaries for the nation that asked itself such questions.

In February 1898 the pro-Dreyfus intellectuals formed the *Ligue des Droits l'Homme et du Citoyen* (League for the Rights of Man and the Citizen). To protest against this, the *Ligue de la Patrie Française* was reorganized at the end of that year. Illustrious academics, famous artists such as Edgar Degas (1834–1919) and Auguste Renoir (1841–1917), and a large portion of the French intellectual establishment signed petitions in support of the army. The *affaire* also left deep and enduring marks on the political left wing. The search for truth had induced them, at great cost, to recognize a contradiction and a problem: even among those who fight against social injustice, the negation of justice can take root and grow; if we wish to eliminate injustice, political struggles alone are not enough.

Anyone who reflects today upon what happened to Captain Dreyfus will come to one fundamental conclusion: having occurred in France, the *affaire* vividly illustrates that legislated tolerance is not enough on its own to ensure peaceful coexistence among different religions, cultures and ethnic groups; such politics are a necessary premise, without which nothing can be achieved, but, as the facts demonstrated, are not of themselves sufficient.

The Birth of the Zionist Movement

While celebrating the centenary of the revolution of 1789, a rabbi expressed the opinion that "fortunately in France today everybody is considered French". In saying this he paid a homage to liberalism and what it had produced. The Alliance Israélite Universelle, as we have seen, also espoused

In Eastern Europe, Jews lived in large, usually poor communities and spoke Yiddish, a language that has produced a flourishing literature. There, where anti-Jewish discrimination was more persistent and explosions of anti-Semitism more frequent, the Jews felt themselves to be not so much a religious minority as one of the many nations that formed the Hapsburg and Tsarist Empires. The majority of these Jewish "nationalists" thought that the problems of their people could only be solved where they lived, through forms of autonomy, especially in the areas of education and culture.

As a reaction to persistent shows of intolerance, which often ended in massacres (as favoured by the Tsarist powers in Russia), another form of Jewish nationalism was born under the name of Zionism. For Zionists, the problems of the Jews could only be solved with the recognition, after millennia, of a Jewish national state. Some identified the "natural" Jewish homeland as Palestine; others, by contrast, maintained that the decisive question was the acquisition of territory — any territory — on which the Jewish state could be founded. With this aim in mind, Zionist leaders made enquiries as to the willingness of countries such as Portugal, Italy and Belgium to cede a portion of their African colonies. In 1903 Theodor Herzl, the founder of the Zionist movement, briefly considered the British proposal to create a "New Palestine" in Africa (the so-called Uganda project, even though it was not in fact in Uganda). Their enemies accused the Zionists of being colonialists.

There is no doubt that when they thought of settlements outside Europe — especially in countries not inhabited by people of European stock — most Zionists reasoned in the same way as most nineteenth-century Europeans: "whites" brought civilization to backward peoples. Nevertheless, the settlements of European

Jews in Palestine — which began in 1878 — quickly assumed a socialist organizational form. The best-known instance of this is the *kibbutz*, a farming colony based on either religious or left-wing ideas in which complete economic and social equality is maintained. The first *kibbutz* was set up in 1910 at Degania.

The Zionist movement, which remained a minority affiliation in Jewish communities of the diaspora until the Nazi extermination camps and even afterwards, was never a political party. It was the proposal of a complete alternative: to found another society elsewhere. The Zionist hypothesis foresaw the creation of a new state and a new settlement, which would be the expression of a new society. The movement contained within itself different and even opposing ideas of how to construct that new society and the new Jewish state.

Zionism represented a part of the Jewish national movement, but it never occupied the "classic" position in the Jewish world that other nationalisms, which are for the most part right-wing movements, have occupied in other cultures. Within Zionism, right-wing, left-wing and centrist positions battled against each other. These positions were neither articulated by a single organization nor the expression of a single political vision, even though they found themselves under the same canopy.

Because of the presence within them of so many different political parties, the Zionist settlements in Palestine have had and continue to have a democratic structure that allows the co-existence of diverse tendencies, even minority proposals to abandon Zionism in favour of the peaceful co-existence of Arabs and Jews in Palestine. ■

Left: postcards celebrating the Jewish New Year. Below: Herzl with two other founders of the movement, in a 1906 sticker representing Zionist aspirations — the Wailing Wall and a farm in Palestine.

Western liberal ideas. Many of the Alliance's members, however, were beginning to be sympathetic to the Zionist movement.

The recognized father-founder of the Zionist movement was the Hungarian journalist and writer Theodor Herzl, whose theoretical work on the necessity of a Jewish homeland — *The Jewish State* — appeared in 1896. He was among the principle organizers of the first Zionist Congress in Basel in 1897. Zionism was one of several late-nineteenth-century responses to the problem that arose from the defence and vindication of Jewish identity and the right to be different. By the end of the previous century, the politics of tolerance already seemed — and to a large extent were — incapable of guaranteeing that right. Thus various responses arose that, despite their differences, had one basic element in common: they were products of the anti-Semitic culture of the period.

The Right to Diversity or Separation?

In the mental universe of the nineteenth century, the idea of the nation — linked to a shared territory, language and culture — played a central role. There were undoubtedly strong nationalist feelings in the mass psychology of the Eastern European Jews; a considerable portion of the Jewish population identified themselves as a "nation". Various proposals arose from this. For some, the solution could be found in the principle of the "right to diversity"; even though they were dispersed among many nations, all Jews must fight for the recognition of their identity in the place they were born, lived,

and would one day die. In the countries of Eastern and Central Europe, many communities sought this kind of solution. Others saw the only possible answer in territorial (and psychological) separation and a completely new start for the Jews in a homeland of their own. These were the Zionists, who were not so much an actual party as a group that shared a particular political, intellectual and moral outlook.

This response, which tends towards divisiveness rather than finding a way for different kinds of people to live together, bore within it the seed of reactionary separatism of the sort that served as the theoretical basis of South Africa's old system of apartheid. Something of that kind was there in the ghetto experience, or at least that is how *Catholic Civilization* interpreted it when discussing the Dreyfus case. In essence, the Jesuits preached that Roman and Medieval thinking on the question of the Jews was the correct road to follow; it was necessary to return to the ghetto and abandon once·and for all the nefarious legacy of the Revolution.

Dreyfus thus became a symbol of modernity in a different way: in spite of himself, he embodied the revolutionary, democratizing principles of 1789.

Top left: Drumont on the front page of his newspaper. Bottom left: two Jewish graves in a German cemetery. Below: water-carriers in Galicia in a photograph from the beginning of the twentieth century.

Chapter 3

FROM **P**ARIS TO **O**DESSA: **A**NTI-SEMITIC **E**UROPE

"POGROM" IS A RUSSIAN WORD THAT EVOKES MASSACRES, VIOLENCE AND DESTRUCTION. IT WAS OFTEN HEARD IN EASTERN EUROPE AND TSARIST RUSSIA. IN THE LEAST AND THE MOST ADVANCED SOCIETIES OF THE OLD CONTINENT, A "CONDITIONED REFLEX" MADE PEOPLE THINK OF THE JEW AS "THE ENEMY WITHIN".

Around the time that Dreyfus was arrested on charges of espionage, two new terms entered the European linguistic heritage: "pogrom" and "anti-Semitism". The first appearance of the latter was in 1879, in a book entitled *Der Sieg des Judentums über des Germanentum* (*The Victory of Judaism over Germanism*), which sold twelve editions in its first year of publication alone. The author was Wilhelm Marr, a German political agitator, former socialist and founder, in the same year, of the *Antisemiten Liga* (the Anti-Semitic League).

Marr's most famous work has a very telling title: *Der Verzweiflungskampf der arischen Völker gegen das Judentum* (*The Desperate Battle of the Aryan Peoples Against Judaism*). It is another example (even in its title) of the logical leaps that make up anti-Semitic "theory". Just as "race" was a conceptual tool forged for specific operations in the field of natural history, so "Semite" and "Aryan" (which came into common use in the 1840s) were terms borrowed from the vocabulary of linguistics. They originally served to distinguish groups of languages of different origins, then gradually came to be applied to other fields and in particular to the ethnic groups who speak those languages. From there it was a small step to a discussion of "Semitic" and "Aryan" peoples, cultures and civilizations. Thus the terms came to be used in a racial sense.

The strong and widespread anti-Jewish substratum

A Jewish peasant of the Carpathian region in a 1920s' photograph.

The resurgence of accusations of ritual homicide is evidence that, while the new anti-Semitism was increasing on the basis of racism, the medieval myths of traditional Christian anti-Jewish sentiment still had firm roots in the collective consciousness.

in European culture produced another conceptual dislocation of the term "Semitic". All the ancient Near East and the entire Arab world were inhabited by peoples who spoke "Semitic" languages. Nevertheless, very soon the term was narrowed to signify only those things that were connected with Jews or Judaism. It was therefore possible to attribute an anti-Jewish racist significance to the term "anti-Semitism", although from an analytic and scientific point of view such an attribution was clearly erroneous. It was probably this very lack of precision that favoured the success of the term. As H. Berding, author of an important study of German anti-Semitism, observed, the term became a hotchpotch concept within which all the anti-Jewish currents — whatever their different motives and objectives — were evident and in unison.

Prejudice Reawakens in the Heart of Europe

Wilhelm Raabe's *The Shepherd of Hunger*, a mid-nineteenth century German novel, enjoyed great popular success. One of its protagonists — a Jew who converts to Christianity and changes his Jewish name — declares: "I have every right to be German when I like and to refuse that honour when it seems convenient to do so... Since they have stopped putting us to death as the poisoners of water-holes and slaughterers of Christian children, our position is decidedly better than yours, the so-called Aryans."

Those words were written in 1864; twenty years later, when the term "anti-Semitism" had already come into common use, they were no longer true. In the 1880s and 1890s, accusations of ritual homicide and butchering children were brought against Jews with renewed vigour. These cases did not arise in non-European communities like Damascus: they arose in Europe itself — in Galicia and Hungary (both governed from Vienna), in Pomerania and the Rhineland, and later, in the early years of the twentieth century, in Tsarist Russia. From the Rhineland to Kiev, the sinister myth of Jews spreading Christian blood on their Passover bread flourished anew.

Sometimes crimes were perpetrated with the sole object of provoking persecution of the Jews. In 1884, in Skurz in Pomerania, the village butcher killed and dismembered a fourteen-year-old boy in order to stir up an anti-Jewish campaign using the pretext of a presumed ritual homicide. Diverse crimes and disappearances were used to anti-Semitic ends. Always, even after the accusations had been proved false, the accused and quite often their fellow Jews had to abandon the places in which these various "affairs" had been staged. The resurgence of accusations of ritual homicide is evidence that, while the new anti-Semitism was growing on the basis of racism, the medieval myths of traditional Christian anti-Jewish sentiment still had firm roots in the collective consciousness.

An anthropological difference in the two forms of discrimination against the Jews has already been briefly indicated: the "traditional" aversion tended to be characteristic of less developed areas and social strata; the "new" anti-Semitism, by contrast, was the province of the better educated, who were influenced by the "scientific" spirit of the age. It must also be observed that in practice, however, modern anti-Semitism not only coexisted with and drew strength from traditional anti-Jewish sentiment but that, in its turn, it offered new and different bases for the traditional hatred of Jews. In the climate of the "new" anti-Semitism, Jews no longer practised ritual homicide because they were followers of a cruel religion that was the enemy of Christianity, but rather because they were evil by "nature".

Left: Polish Jewish children in front of their school.
Above: a street in the city of Lublin, one of the largest settlements of the Jewish community in Eastern Europe, at the beginning of the century.

Elected by a Very Large Majority

At the end of the nineteenth century, Vienna was the centre of the Hapsburg Empire, which, though in decline, still ranked among the most important European powers; a cosmopolitan city, contributing to all the fields of art and science; a cultural centre of the highest level. There, in that hothouse of culture and thought, one of the decisive intellectual revolutions of our time was born: psychoanalysis.

In 1895 the splendid and glittering capital elected a mayor named Karl Lueger, then leader of the Christian Socialist Party. Eleven years earlier he had been elected a member of parliament, making good use of two developments at that time in Austria: the extension of the electorate in 1882 to include artisans, small businessmen and the lower middle class in general, and the aftermath of two sensational trials for ritual homicide that had taken place in Galicia and Hungary (afflicting a community of two million Jews who were dispersed among the various provinces of the Empire).

In 1882, the Ritter and Tisza-Elzar "affairs" exploded, one after the other. The first was a case of dark deeds, perhaps motivated by passion, which were then used to anti-Semitic ends; the second case was built upon the disappearance of a girl who drowned accidentally. Both these *affaires* ended (after trials, appeals, and new trials) with the acquittal of the accused and proof that the accusations of ritual homicide had been groundless and absurd. The damage, however, had already been done: the anti-Semitic virus had regained its strength, and Lueger made good use of it.

He was at this point the undisputed leader of the anti-Semites in the Hapsburg Empire, and in 1895 he was elected mayor of Vienna by a very large majority. This demonstrates that the middle strata of Viennese society — in particular the artisans — accepted the idea that the Jews (capitalists *par excellence*) were the cause of their troubles. Workers in the Austrian capital were also receptive to the anti-Jewish message.

The success of Lueger was no passing fad: his support lasted a long time, despite the opposition of the government — the executive twice refused to ratify his election as administrative head of the capital. Nevertheless, the electorate voted for Lueger again at subsequent polls, and he was mayor until his death in 1910. For fifteen years, then, Vienna — one of the political and cultural capitals of Europe — was administered by a man who flew the flag of anti-Semitism, a man whom Hitler honoured with a warm posthumous homage.

Relations with the municipal administration and services became difficult for Viennese Jews. That they did not suffer more was due to the government's unflinching rebuttal of every attempt to return to anti-Jewish discrimination, such as Lueger's proposal to separate Jewish pupils from other children in primary schools.

A Wave of Pogroms Sweeps over Eastern Europe

In 1878 a Christian Socialist Party also sprang up in Germany, with the support of Chancellor Otto Eduard Leopold von Bismarck. At its head was Adolf Stöcker, who was vehemently anti-Jewish. The Jews, he declared, had purely materialist aspirations and were inherently destructive. Marr, "inventor" of the term anti-Semitism, founded the Anti-Semitic League the following year. Its members boycotted the Jews: nothing could be bought from or sold to them.

Anti-Semitic associations modelled after the League sprang up in many cities. Students also had an anti-Semitic association: its members were forbidden to have any friendly or business contact with Jews; they considered it a duty to insult them, both within and out-

Top left: Alexander III, Tsar of all the Russias from 1881 to 1894, who established an authoritarian government and promoted the persecution of the Jews. Bottom left: Karl Lueger, mayor of Vienna from 1895 to 1910. Below: The Feast of the Triumph of the Law at the Synagogue of Leghorn, an 1850 painting by Solomon Alexander Hart.

side the universities, and to provoke them to fight duels.

In 1880 Stöcker presented a petition to the government, for which he collected 225,000 signatures, asking that restrictions be placed on Jewish immigration into the German Empire, that Jews be dismissed from all types of government jobs, and that they be forbidden to work as teachers. It is no coincidence that this programme was, in its essence, adopted by Hitler in the first years of his dictatorship.

In 1881 there were many instances of anti-Semitic violence in Pomerania. In September 1892 an international anti-Semitic congress was held in Dresden. It included representatives from Germany, the Austro-Hungarian Empire and Russia, where a wave of pogroms was sweeping the land. The congress ended with the decision to found an international anti-Semitic party which would promote the repeal in all nations of laws emancipating the Jews. The Skurz "affair", in which the village butcher killed the boy, followed in 1884. In 1887, for the first time, a member of parliament was elected on an explicitly anti-Semitic platform: Otto Böckel, the author of an anti-Semitic publication of which nearly two million copies were printed. Two years later another anti-Semitic congress was held, this time at Bochum. In 1890 Böckel went on to found the *Antisemitische Volkspartei* (The Popular Anti-Semitic Party), which won four seats (with 48,000 votes out of 7,000,000). In 1891 another accusation of ritual homicide was made at Xanten in the Rhineland, which resulted in yet another scandal. In 1893 the *Antisemitische Volkspartei* won 260,000 votes and sixteen seats in parliament. This electoral success marked the zenith of anti-Semitic agitation in Germany before the advent of Nazism.

Left: mass graves are dug for the burial of the victims of a pogrom in the city of Odessa. Below: the German composer Richard Wagner (1813–83).

A Disturbing Example: Richard Wagner

After 1893 anti-Semitic agitation went into a decline. This was partly due to protests within German society. In 1890 an association to fight against anti-Semitism was founded by a group of educated people; within one year the membership rose to 12,000, and the association became an active and vocal presence, holding conferences and writing editorials in the press. The Social Democratic Party also participated in the battle against anti-Semitism. In 1891 the International Socialist Congress in Brussels condemned anti-Semitism and proclaimed that for the working class there were no rivalries of race, religion or nationality.

Although the most violent expressions of anti-Semitism had declined, anti-Semitism itself had by no means disappeared: rather it had been placed on the back burner because, in the last decade of the nineteenth century, Europe was entering the age of the great imperialist conflicts. The ancient fears and rancours upon which anti-Semitism was based thus found other means of expression.

Nevertheless, anti-Jewish sentiment was still alive and well. This comes as no surprise, and not only because the hatred of Jews was and is a deep structure of "Christian" feeling. With a kind of symbolic

aptness, the umpteenth accusation of ritual homicide was made in 1900, this time in Konitz in Pomerania.

Nineteenth-century Germany had seen the development of an entire anti-Semitic culture that was not the product of a small or marginal school of thought but rather that of important — sometimes central — public figures of the period. Perhaps the most disturbing case is that of Richard Wagner, one of the most important figures in the history of music. In 1850 Wagner published *Das Judentum in der Musik* (*Judaism in Music*). Its content and tone are well represented by the following passage: "It is unnecessary to give proof of the Jewification of modern art; the fact is plain to see. The most important thing is to emancipate ourselves from Jewish oppression."

Thirty years later another central figure of German cultural life, Heinrich von Treitschke, a nationalist historian with idealist leanings, entered the fray against the Jews. In 1879, at the beginning of the

REASON CAN GAIN NO GROUND WITH THE ANTI-SEMITE

The following bitter observations on the persistence of anti-Semitic prejudice as a kind of epidemic were made by the German philologist and historian Theodor Mommsen (1817–1903), winner of the Nobel Prize for Literature in 1902.

You are mistaken if you think that reason can help in this connection. I, too, at one time believed that, and I never stopped protesting against the monstrous infamy that is called anti-Semitism. But it does no good. It is all in vain. All I can give you — all that can be said in general on this ques-

tion — are reasons, logical and moral arguments. But anti-Semites take no notice of such arguments. They only listen to the voice of their own hatred, their own envy, their infamous

instincts. For them, nothing else matters. They are deaf to reason, rights and morality. One cannot act upon them... There is no protection against the rabble, be it on the street or in the drawing-room: a mob is a mob, and anti-Semitism is the conviction of the mob. It is like a terrible epidemic, like cholera; one can neither explain it nor cure it. ∎

Theodor Mommsen to Hermann Bahr, in H. Bahr, *Der Antisemitimus. Ein International Interview* (Berlin, 1894), edited by H. Greive, Königstein, 1979, p 27.

most acute phase of the anti-Semitic campaign in Germany, he published *Unsere Aussichten* (*Our Prospects*). It affirmed the unbridgeable distance between "the Germanic being" and "the Oriental being" (the Jews, for him, were Orientals) and evoked the spectre of Jewish domination, to be exercised by the sons of "the herd of underwear merchants born in Poland", who were destined to become the controllers of the stock exchange and the German press. The response of the great classicist Theodor Mommsen was severe. He also acknowledged a "difference... between the German Occidental and those of Semitic blood", and for this reason he strongly advised the Jews to take the path of assimilation. Nevertheless, Mommsen refuted Treitschke's arguments and accused him of having removed the garment of modesty from anti-Semitism and made it "respectable".

Top left: in this cartoon a capitalist is being squashed by Karl Marx's Das Kapital.
Bottom left: Theodor Mommsen, German philologist and historian.
Above: Portrait of a Boy, by the late-nineteenth-century Hungarian painter Isidore Kaufmann.

"I am Delighted When Jews are Killed"

Neither Wagner nor Treitschke had anything to do with the crude "science" that sought to explain racial superiority by means of biology. Nor did the third figure in this little gallery of German anti-Semitic culture: Werner Sombart, one of the founders of modern economic history. In 1911 he published *Die Juden und das Wirtschaftsleben* (*Jews and Economic Life*). Its thesis was new: it was a reworking of the economic anti-Semitism of the early socialist movement, in which capitalism and Jewishness are seen as effectively identical. The following year, Sombart published *Die Zukunft der Juden* (*The Future of the Jews*). Here the perspective broadens: Sombart sees Jewish superiority in every area of national life. What could be done?

For Sombart, the Jews are a necessary yeast in the economy and society; nevertheless, he maintains that, "We don't want a mash, half white and half black." Nothing remained but to invoke a kind of racial segregation, a complete separation, imposed by the

The market square of Moscow in a photograph taken at the beginning of the twentieth century.

effectively "inferior" majority on a "superior" minority. This theme of the presumed superiority of the Jews thus carried the most violent strain of the anti-Jewish virus.

It was in this context that Friedrich Neitzsche wrote, "I have not yet met a single German who felt goodwill towards the Jews." According to Neitzsche, the Jews were a people who deserved to be recognized, since "it was Jewish free-thinkers, scholars and doctors who held aloft the standard of enlightenment and spiritual independence, at the cost of the most painful personal constriction." It was perhaps the ultimate expression of the German lack of goodwill towards Jews that Neitzsche's brother-in-law, Bernard Förster, popularized his work by imposing upon it an anti-Semitic interpretation. He was able to do this because Neitzsche was himself essentially a child of

his times and his fatherland when he justified his admiration for the Jews by referring to their "blood".

From the second half of the nineteenth century to the beginning of the twentieth, the role of "high" culture in the German aversion to the Jews is also one of the keys to understanding the sociology of the militant anti-Semitism of the period. Research has shown that it was a phenomenon of the city rather than the countryside, of indifferent rather than of pious Christians, and apparently of the educated strata of society.

In the nineteenth century the largest Jewish community in the world lived in the Russian Empire (which included a large part of Poland). According to the Census of 1897, the only one taken before the 1917 Revolution, the Tsar had over 5,000,000 Jewish subjects. Most of them worked as artisans, in small businesses (especially in the textile sector), in commerce (often on a small

On 6 April 1903, there was a pogrom in Russia that deeply shocked European public opinion. It happened on the first day of the Easter holiday in the Orthodox Church and the seventh day of the Jewish Passover, in a city with a Jewish community of 50,000 people.

scale), and as factory workers. In the mid-1880s a government commission revealed that ninety per cent of the Jews in Russia were extremely poor and lived wretchedly; the report concludes, "It is obvious that the condition of the Jews is insupportable."

Six hundred and fifty "laws of exception" — restricting their freedoms or diminishing their rights — were brought to bear on this suffering humanity. Even so, deep-rooted traditional anti-Jewish sentiment made sure that social tensions and frustrations were vented upon the Jews. Thus, in Russia, anti-Semitic campaigns were orchestrated from above and tolerated by the authorities. "To tell the truth, I myself am delighted when the Jews are killed", declared Alexander III, Tsar of all the Russias from 1881 to 1894.

The Destructive Fury Explodes

The first explosion of "popular" fury against the Jews was in Odessa in 1871, but from 1881 to 1889 there was a sustained wave of anti-Semitic violence: attacks upon the Jews were recorded in twenty-six different places. After a brief hiatus it began again: between 1902 and 1906 there was a succession of brutal attacks against the Jews in another twenty-one places. These explosions of anti-Jewish violence — which were, for the most part, directed from above — were called by a new name: *pogrom*, a Russian word that is usually translated as "destruction". The word, however, is part of a lexical group whose meanings also comprise "thunder", "fury" and "annihilation of the enemy". *Pogrom* thus denotes an explosion of destructive fury aimed at annihilating the Jewish "enemy".

In 1903 there was a pogrom in Kisinev that deeply shocked European public opinion. It happened on 6

April, the first day of the Easter holiday for Orthodox Christians and the seventh day of the Jewish Passover, in a city with a Jewish community of 50,000 people. The pretext was the suicide of a Christian girl; according to the pro-government press, this was the fault of her Jewish employer. The agitation of the press united with the more insidious efforts of the authorities, in particular those of a high-ranking police officer who was the direct emissary of the government. For two days the Jews of Kisinev were at the mercy of a ferocious mob that killed and wounded, threw babies out of windows, raped women, tortured, put out eyes, sacked houses and shops, and set fire to synagogues. In the final count there were fifty dead, one hundred wounded, and almost a thousand homes destroyed.

In the second half of the nineteenth century the vast phenomenon of anti-Semitism assumed diverse forms, arose in various areas, and involved places and cultures that were quite different from one another. But in each of these cases immediate superficial causes can be found. The emancipation that put Jew and non-Jew in more direct and open competition is one true cause, but it is not "universal": the Russian Jews were far from being emancipated, as witnessed by the incredible number of "laws of exception" to which they were subjected. Certainly, in general, in the course of the nineteenth century Jews everywhere abandoned their

Left: the New Ghetto of Venice today. At the beginning of the seventeenth century this area, which borders on the Old Ghetto, reflected the expansion of the whole portion of Venice inhabited by the Jews.
Below: The Seder (Passover Supper) in a mid-eighteenth-century print.

traditional status. They emigrated; they created a new culture with a language of their own (Yiddish); they studied in non-Jewish schools as well as those reserved for Jews; and they founded political organizations (for the most part on the left, especially in places where they still had to fight for equal rights). Some of them also enjoyed social and economic success. In the German Jewish community, as we shall see, the largest stratum was what we would today define as "middle class".

A Sort of "Conditioned Reflex"

In Germany as elsewhere, a conspicuous part of the Jewish community used the opportunities offered by emancipation to study and to enter the liberal professions. Essentially this was the result of the combination of three elements: the urban character of the Jewish minorities (institutions of higher education were concentrated in the cities); the desire for upward social mobility of a minority whose aspirations had long been thwarted; and the specific tradition of the Jews, a "bookish people" for whom study and culture had always been regarded as positive values.

There was also their economic success, in certain respects greater than that of other groups.

In 1908, fifty-five of the 200 millionaires in Prussia were Jews, of whom thirty-three were from the finance and banking sector. This was clearly a high proportion considering the size of the Jewish community in relation to the general population. Jewish "millionaires", however, were in no way representative of the entire Jewish community or even of the majority of Jews.

In Germany and Russia, as in France, particular causes were interwoven with the general causes. In 1873, for example,

the German Empire was shaken by a stock market crash. Enriched by war reparations paid by France after their defeat at the hands of Germany in 1870, the Germans went on a sort of financial and industrial spending spree. Stock companies sprang up like mushrooms, and great building projects were started in the cities. It was an extravagant binge, and it nourished stock market speculation that eventually led to financial catastrophe, largely at the expense of the middle classes.

What better scapegoat than the Jew? Since Jews were represented in greater proportion than others among the financiers and stockholders of great enterprises, who else could be responsible? The mental mechanism was always the same: an unjustified generalization. If anyone was to blame it was single financiers

Left: a view of the ghetto in Rome at the end of the nineteenth century.
Above; a Jewish baker in the Marais quarter of Paris in the 1930s.

and groups of speculators; whether or not they were Jews is beside the point.

Many other such examples could be provided, but to do so would be to describe the same phenomenon over and over again, and above all to risk creating an erroneous attitude that "justifies" the hatred of the Jews: certainly that hatred was unjust, but it was given "foundation" by the nature and extent of what was happening. Besides, if we penetrate further into the maze of single circumstances we might well lose sight of the heart of the matter: that people of the most contrasting cultures, of the most diverse economic, social and political conditions, and for a variety of different reasons, recognized in the Jew the ultimate cause of their own difficulties. This was due to something more profound than a single motive or a constellation of circumstances. And it is significant that this sort of "conditioned reflex" acted both in less developed societies and in those that were socially and economically advanced.

The latter case is the more disturbing. There was and is something called "reactionary modernism": a way of thinking that is widespread in Germany but also present

The Jewish quarter of Amsterdam in a 1875 print.

elsewhere. It combines a positive attitude to science and technology — and thus to industrial development and the distribution of the goods it produces (trains, cars, planes, and so on) — with contempt for reason, especially in politics. This contempt has often been justified by invoking a love of novelty that entails the rejection of current aesthetic values; this in turn may become a fascination with horror and violence as welcome antidotes to bourgeois boredom and decadence. According to the "reactionary modernists", democracy — with its proclamations of equality and its need for mediation between differing opinions — is the clearest expression of that boredom and decadence. In other words, democracy is boring and decadent because it employs reason in the political arena.

In place of reason, the reactionary modernists value "authenticity", which they define in absolute terms such as "blood", "race" and "spirit" — these exist in themselves, beyond any need for justification or rational reflection. From this point of view, reason itself is *lebensfeindlich* (hostile to life). It is therefore not difficult for them to embrace anti-Semitism, and they do so.

Chapter 4

THE EXTRAORDINARY
SUCCESS OF A FORGERY

IN 1920 RUMOURS OF A JEWISH-MASONIC PLOT BEGAN TO SPREAD ONCE AGAIN. THESE RUMOURS HAD FORMIDABLE POWER AS PROPAGANDA. *THE TIMES* UPHELD THE AUTHENTICITY OF *THE PROTOCOLS OF THE ELDERS OF ZION*, A LIBELLOUS DOCUMENT THAT WAS EVENTUALLY PROVEN TO BE A FORGERY.

On 8 May 1920, *The Times* published an article under the headline "The Jewish Peril. A Disturbing Pamphlet: A Call for Inquiry". In it, *The Times* upheld the authenticity of a libellous publication and what it "revealed": that there was a secret Jewish global organization whose objective was to establish Jewish global domination by means of democratic, radical, socialist and Communist ideas. A pamphlet put out by this secret and diabolical association constituted the proof of its existence and aims. However, no one knew how the pamphlet had been brought to light or by whom. Furthermore, no one was able to define what the pamphlet actually constituted. The written account of a speech? A report? A manifesto? Something else?

The pamphlet in question became known throughout the world as *The Protocols of the Elders of Zion*. There is no doubt that *The Times* was the main vehicle of its dissemination. This was observed at the time in *La vielle France* by Urban Gohier, a well-known French anti-Semite who in his youth had been of the pro-Dreyfus camp because he was an anti-militarist. It was also clearly stated by one of the heralds of Italian anti-Semitism, Giovanni Preziosi: in the preface to his translation of *The Protocols* in 1921, Preziosi wrote that the authority of *The Times* had drawn the attention of scholars and politicians to the pamphlet, so that public opinion had been stirred, all copies of the

*T*his fiendish and threatening figure, sporting a Star of David on his chest, is a stereotypical representation of the so-called "Jewish lobby" about to destroy American democracy, as shown in an anti-Semitic propaganda poster of the 1920s.

pamphlet had sold out, and further editions had to be printed.

The pamphlet had first appeared in Russia in an abridged version in 1902; it was reprinted in the version that was destined to become famous in 1905. It was included in the twelfth chapter of *The Great in the Small, the Antichrist as an Imminent Political Possibility* by Sergei Alexandrovich Nilus, an ultra-Orthodox religious fanatic; this book was published by Czarskoï Selo, the Imperial residence near St Petersburg. In the years that followed various editions of the pamphlet were published, but the real boom in sales occurred after the October Revolution. Between 1918 and 1920 many reprints were circulated among the Whites who were fighting against the Bolsheviks, often in abridged or simplified forms. In those same years the pamphlet was disseminated among the first wave of Russian emigrants and translated into various languages. In 1919 the first German and Polish versions appeared; in 1920 the first English version appeared in London and Boston, the first French version in Paris, and the first Hungarian version in Vienna. The following year it was translated into Italian and Serbian.

From then onwards it became a worldwide best seller. It is difficult, however, to trace its dissemination. Often editions appeared without any indication of the place or date of publication. Moreover, after 1945 sales of the pamphlet went underground: rather than being displayed in shop windows, it was sold under the counter. It was circulated discreetly, sometimes secretly. Nevertheless, it continued to be read in Europe, North America and South America, and was a great success in the Arab world. In 1958 the Egyptian President Gamal Abd el Nasser recommended it to an eminent Indian journalist as essential reading for an understanding of global politics. In 1974 King Faisal of Saudi Arabia sent copies as gifts to the French Foreign Minister Michel Jobert and the Italian

Foreign Minister Aldo Moro. Libyan President Qaddafi usually gives it as a present to his guests. The reason for all this can be found in the preface of a 1957 edition of *The Protocols*, published in Cairo in the "political books" series put out by the Information Service of the United Arab Republic. According to the anonymous writer of the preface, *The Protocols* is "the most important and dangerous Zionist document".

Left: Nicholai Romanov, Tsar Nicholas II of Russia from 1894 to 1917.
Below: the cover of the French edition of the Protocols, published in Vichy in 1943.

Who Wrote *The Protocols*?

On 12 May 1920, four days after the original *Times* article, an anti-Bolshevik review circulated among the Russian expatriate community published the testimony of Alexandre du Chayla. Of French origin, he was a former captain of Cossacks who fought against the Communist Revolution. He had met Nilus while studying at the Theological Academy of St Petersburg.

Du Chayla's version of events then appeared in various publications on both sides of the Atlantic. He claimed that Nilus had shown him the manuscript of *The Protocols*. Much to the amazement of Nilus, the text had not made a strong impression upon du Chayla: in fact, he had thought it "a very close relative of the pamphlets of Edouard Drumont and of the great hoax of Léo Taxil". The latter was known for having made an astounding revelation: a Jewish-Masonic plot was threatening religion, social order, and decent living; the leaders of this conspiracy had a system of telephonic communication — devised and operated by devils — that allowed them to keep in permanent contact with the seven principal capitals of the world.

Nilus had assured du Chayla that *The Protocols* was French and must have been written by the secretary of an international organization of highly-placed Jews. However, du Chayla observed that it contained "errors of

UN PRÉTENDU FAUX VERIDIQUE

LES PROTOCOLES DES SAGES DE SION

PAR
JEAN DE LA HERSE

ÉDITÉ PAR "LA PORTE LATINE"
126 BOULEVARD DES BATIGNOLLES
PRIX 8 FRANCS
N° 4

Top right: Giovanni Preziosi, a bitter Italian anti-Semite of the Fascist period and the Republic of Salò, who popularized The Protocols *in Italy. On 25 April 1945 he committed suicide. Bottom right: the Irish writer George Bernard Shaw (1856–1950).*

spelling and, above all, of grammar that were not French". Finally, the former captain of Cossacks suggested a link between *The Protocols* and the activities of the Tsarist secret police in Paris.

The Work of the Tsarist Secret Police

A similar suggestion was made by another Russian expatriate, according to *The Times* correspondent in Constantinople in 1921. At that point, a little over a year after the launch of the English translation of *The Protocols*, *The Times* made a public retraction. In a lengthy correspondence from Constantinople in August 1921, the "most influential newspaper in the world" (as Britian's chief rabbi called it, after the paper's umpteenth attack on the Jews) informed its readers that *The Protocols* was largely copied from Maurice Joly's 1865 pamphlet against Napoleon III, *Dialogues aux enfers entre Montesquieu et Machiavel* (*Dialogues Between Montesquieu and Machiavelli in Hell*). Historians demonstrated the extent of the debt *The Protocols* owed to Joly's pamphlet. The arrange-

THE CONTENT OF *THE PROTOCOLS* ACCORDING TO *THE TIMES*

1. There is, as there has been for centuries, an international political organization of Jews; 2. It appears that the motivation of this organization is a traditional eternal hatred of Christianity and a titanic ambition to rule the world; 3. The end to which this organization has aimed through the centuries is the destruction of the nation states and the substitution of international Jewish domination; 4. The method used to weaken and destroy the existent political states is the injection of ideas that will lead to their disintegration by a process well-judged by liberalism and radicalism, then by socialism and Communism, and finally by anarchy, the *reductio ad absurdam* of egalitarian principles. At the same time, Israel will remain undamaged by these corrosive doctrines...; 5. The political dogmas that evolve in Christian Europe, her politics and her democratic constitutions are all equally despised by the wise elders of Israel. For them, government is a sublime and secret art, acquired through traditional culture and practised by a very small elite in some hidden sanctuary...; 6. In this conception of government, the masses are no more than a wretched herd; and the political agitators of the *goyim* (gentiles), who are as blind as the flocks they lead, are simply puppets in the hands of the elders of Israel: they are mostly corrupt, always impotent, easily manipulated by flattery, threat or blackmail for the ends of Jewish domination; 7. The press, the theatre, the Stock Exchange, science, the law, in the hands of those who hold all the world's wealth, are furthermore instruments to stir up public opinion, to demoralize the young, to promote vice among the general population, to destroy idealistic aspirations (Christian culture), to establish a cult of cash, of materialist skepticism, of the cynical appetite for pleasure. ∎

From *The Times*, 8 May 1920.

ment of the text was inspired by the *Dialogues*, as was at least forty per cent of the text itself. In nine chapters, the "borrowings" constitute over half and sometimes as much as three-quarters of the text. "Protocol VII" is copied verbatim. By this time others had seriously questioned the authenticity of *The Protocols*.

A review of the German version of *The Protocols* appeared in a Berlin magazine in May 1920. It told another interesting story, and brought evidence to prove it: *The Protocols* was a reworking of part of a German novel published in 1868. (In that year a law had been passed conceding the first stages of emancipation to the Jews, and a violent anti-Semitic reaction had followed.) The novel was entitled *Biarritz* and was written by Sir John Retcliffe, the pseudonym of Hermann Goedsche. Goedsche had been a functionary in the Prussian postal service, but was dismissed for fraud perpetrated against a Jew. He then became a journalist and writer.

The book contains a chapter entitled "In the Jewish Cemetery in Prague". It portrays a midnight meeting of representatives of the tribes of Israel, in which a plot is hatched to free the Jews from all kinds of discrimination and, moreover, to establish the grandsons of those present as the future princes of the earth and rulers of all the nations. This part of the novel, rewritten and published separately, was a significant contribution to the anti-Semitic literature of the time. Its ideas and images resurfaced in *The Protocols*.

In May 1920 there was thus already proof that *The Protocols* was a forgery. This gives rise to at least three questions. Why did *The Times* endorse *The Protocols*? Why did the newspaper allow a

There were many Jews among the Russian revolutionaries, and in fact they were more numerous in proportion than any other nationality. This, however, has nothing to do with the spectral 'Jewish plot'.

year to elapse before publishing a retraction? And why did *The Protocols* continue to be disseminated everywhere even after it became obvious that it was a complete fabrication, probably the work of the Tsarist secret police?

On 3 January 1920 Winston Churchill, Minister for War of His Majesty's Government of Great Britain, attacked pacifists in a speech in Sutherland, in which he claimed that "they want to destroy every religious faith... they believe in the Soviet internationale of the Russian and Polish Jews". The future Prime Minister of Britain was fully immersed in a sort of collective psychosis; the same mechanism was operating in 1920, in nations that feared contagion from the Soviet Revolution, as had operated during the wave of anarchist activity at the end of the nineteenth century. In both cases, the spectre was that of a "Jewish plot".

Is it not true, asked those obsessed by the phantom of Jewish conspiracy, that the German imperial government allowed Lenin to pass over its territory on his way from Switzerland to Russia in order to start the Communist Revolution? And isn't it true that the majority of leading Bolsheviks are Jews? What is more, is it not true that, once in power, the Bolsheviks made a separate peace with Germany? Some read this move as a plot engineered by German Jewish bankers; others saw it as an even more sophisticated intrigue aimed at sweeping away all the major Western capitalist governments. In the end, nothing would be left but Jewish domination of the world. And all this was foretold in the "prophetic" *Protocols*.

This loose list of events had nothing to do with reality, even though some of its major elements, considered in isolation, were based in fact.

Anti-Semitic Propaganda under New Management

There were many Jews among the Russian revolutionaries; in fact they were more numerous in proportion than any other nationality within the all-encompassing imperial entity of Tsarist Russia. This, however, has nothing to do with the spectral "Jewish plot": many Jews in the Russian Empire were poor (the gutter press of the period called them *luftmenchen*, "men who live on air"), and most were subjected to myriads of oppressive and discriminatory measures.

In 1919 a Jewish newspaper in Britain tried — while sticking to the facts — to explain this flourishing myth of the Russian Revolution as a Jewish plot. By that time the anti-Semitic campaign in various European countries had already passed into the hands of the press and government information and security services. According to the Jewish newspaper, the best way for these parties to raise public indignation against Bolshevism was to represent it as Jewish.

Fifty-five years later the historian A. Sutton, discussing the aid that US finance gave to the young Soviet state, confirmed the substance of that explanation: according to Sutton, the insistence with which the myth of the Jewish plot was disseminated suggests that it might have been a strategy to distract

Left: a Bolshevik poster inciting opposition to the White Army. Below: Pope Benedict XV.

The proof that

The Protocols *was a*

forgery became for the

anti-Semite the ultimate

proof of its authenticity.

public attention from the real problems and true causes of social tension.

There is something amazing about the mental universe of the anti-Semite. His outlook can be summarized as follows: the Jew is the devil, and the devil's power rests partially if not completely in his ability to hide this power from mankind. Besides, popular wisdom tells us that "there is no smoke without fire". In this way, the proof that *The Protocols* was a forgery became for the anti-Semite the ultimate proof of its authenticity. The Catholic prelate Monsignor Ernest Jouin — founder and editor of *Revue internationale des sociétés secrètes* — did not hesitate to espouse this point of view. And he was praised by the Vatican Secretary of State, Cardinal Pietro Gasparri, and by Pope Benedict XV for his struggle against "enemy sects". Jouin was also the editor of *The Protocols* in France. In 1921, confronted with the proof that *The Protocols* was a forgery, he had no doubts: "The Jews fight against *The Protocols*, first with suppression and then with denial. That double attitude induces us to believe in the authenticity of this famous document; and, in any case, to feel absolutely certain of its veracity. Israel is entangled in its own nets."

As Giovanni Preziosi maintained, doubts as to the authenticity of *The Protocols* did not put its veracity in doubt. Hitler was to agree with him:

"[*The Protocols*] expounds clearly and consciously that which many Jews desire unconsciously. This is important. It is immaterial which Jewish brain conceived these revelations; what is decisive is that they reveal, with a precision that makes us shudder, the character and activities of the Jewish people and, with all their ramifications, the ultimate ends to which they tend."

Despite the demonstration of its complete falsity, *The Protocols* continue to be read even today. In 1988, Hamas — the Islamic fundamentalist organization that uses terrorism to undermine and oppose the peace process between the Palestinians and the

Israelis — published its "Fundamental Paper". This document maintains that the true and ultimate aims of Zionism are summarized in *The Protocols of the Elders of Zion*. And yet it is well known nowadays that *The Protocols* was fabricated by some official of the Tsarist secret police in Paris at the end of the nineteenth century, at the height of the Dreyfus affair, who used as his sources — and sometimes copied outright — passages from an anti-Semitic novel and an attack on Napoleon III.

Left: Lev Davidovich Bronstein, better known as Trotsky, Commissar of Internal Affairs after the Bolsheviks took power in Russia.
Below: a synagogue in Cairo, devastated after an anti-Jewish attack in 1945.

HISTORY IN THE NIGHTMARES OF ANTI-SEMITES

As an example of the persistent success of The Protocols, *there follows a passage from a preface written by A. Nuwaihid to the Lebanese edition of 1967. From 1940 to 1944, Nuwaihid had been the director of Arabic Radio Broadcasting in Palestine under the mandate.*

World Judaism is a Satanic "force" in the form of a secret organization, but is at the same time both open and hidden. The organization has taken the form of a viper, and this viper has a programme composed of nine stages leading to its final goal. The programme was initiated at the time of the Jewish exile from Babylon, twenty-four or twenty-five centuries ago. The last stage will be enacted at the end of the twentieth century in Palestine. Such is their ambition! [...] In thirty years' time the Jewish programme will culminate in Palestine via Constantinople. The eighth stage was in 1917 in Russia. The Jewish plot has attempted simultaneously to destroy the Russian Orthodox Church, the Papacy, and Islam. The seventh stage, according to the Jewish programme, was accomplished in St. Petersburg in 1881 when Tsar Alexander II was assassinated by the bombs of the "Lovers of Zion". The sixth stage was in 1871, after the war between Germany and France, in consequence of which the map of Europe was changed. Notice that there were two stages in a mere ten years! The fifth stage began in London in 1814, just before the fall of Napoleon. The fourth stage took place in Paris in 1790, just before Napoleon came on the scene. Let me reiterate that the viper accomplished four stages over the course of 127 years, from 1790 to 1917. The third stage took place in 1552 in Madrid, after the expulsion of the Jews from Spain and Portugal, which had been the headquarters from which they sought to dominate the world. The second stage was around the year 69 AD in Rome at the time of Caesar Augustus [sic]. The first stage was in 429 BC in Greece. The Jews were then under Persian domination in Palestine, a century before the arrival of Alexander the Great. (The head of the snake represents the leaders, the initiated of Israel. It penetrates into the heart of every nation to corrupt and destroy it; having come from Zion, it must return there after having accomplished its cycle of conquests. The Zionists have long ago drawn the map on which the reptile's journey is traced, and on that map are marked the great stages that have been accomplished, and those yet to be accomplished.)

From R. Neher-Bernheim 'Le bestseller actuel de la littérature antisémite: le Protocoles des Sages de Sion', in P. A. Tanguieff, Les Protocoles des Sages de Sion, *Berg International, 1992, pp. 392–3.* ∎

Chapter 5

JEWS IN THE
NEW **W**ORLDS

IN THE UNITED STATES, WHERE THE LARGEST JEWISH COMMUNITY IN THE WORLD FLOURISHES, ANTI-SEMITISM IS BASED ON CULTURAL DISCRIMINATION. NOT EVEN THE SOVIET UNION WAS IMMUNE TO THIS PREJUDICE: STALIN USED IT AS A TERRIBLE WEAPON IN HIS POLITICAL STRUGGLES.

In the nineteenth and twentieth centuries Jews had to adapt to the new world of liberalism and emancipation, but they also explored other "new worlds".

The first was the geographical New World: America (especially North America). In 1840 there were no more than 15,000 Jews in the United States; twenty years later there were ten times that number; and by 1880 there were almost 300,000. Between 1899 and 1914 about two million Jews crossed the Atlantic. The first wave was made up largely of German Jews, the second of Jews from Eastern Europe, especially the Tsarist Empire.

In the early nineteenth century the United States took heed of the European stereotype of the cunning and too-capable Jew: Jews were subject to legal discrimination in the USA as well. As a juridically Christian country, the thirteen original states had laws — which were considered constitutional — limiting the rights of Jews to vote and hold public office. These laws were not repealed until after the Civil War of 1861–65.

Some Jews in the first wave of immigrants were involved in the Californian gold rush of 1848–50, but as entrepreneurs and artisans rather than prospectors. Some made fortunes, such as Levi Strauss, the inventor of blue jeans. A minority became rich more rapidly than others, such as the Irish and the Italians, who had immigrated into the United States at about the same time. At first the hostility shown to Jews was the same

A religious ceremony in a New York synagogue.

as that shown to these other groups: it was the antipathy of the long-established towards the newcomer, and was thus not specifically anti-Jewish.

In general terms, the population of the United States had always been organized in a complex hierarchy defined by two rigid boundaries: at the top was the founding group of WASPs (white Anglo-Saxon Protestants) and their descendants, and at the bottom was another long-established group — black slaves and their descendants. On the intermediate rungs of the ladder, the most recently arrived immigrants usually occupied the lowest position, even though their discarded cultures were important for the WASPs. Each group had to become "Americanized" before it could climb up the social ladder. Americanization did not entail the renunciation of religious faith

or anything else: freedom of conscience, as enshrined in the Constitution, was a cornerstone of American ideology. Nevertheless, Americanization, everyone agreed, was a process that took some time.

The first signs of specifically anti-Jewish sentiment soon began to appear. In 1876, for example, a hotel on the New Jersey coast announced in the New York newspapers that it did not accept Jewish guests. The following year a hotelier who was destined to become famous — John Hilton — denied a Jewish millionaire entry to his hotel in Saratoga. Rich Jews were quick to react: they bought several hotels in Saratoga. The seaside resorts of the East Coast were thus divided into "Christian" resorts and

"Jewish" resorts. By the beginning of the twentieth century Jews were excluded from many associations and clubs. One famous case, which sparked off a lively debate, was that of a club founded by the head librarian of New York, from which "people with contagious illnesses, invalids and Jews" were excluded.

Left: Levi Strauss, the inventor of blue jeans. Below: the Jewish banker Schiff.

A Society in Rapid Transformation

What was developing in the United States was not, however, economic anti-Semitism: although there was a Jewish economic elite, most Jews in the United States lived in poverty or in only modest social and economic conditions. Of the two million Eastern European Jews who emigrated to the United States between 1899 and 1914, sixty-six per cent could be described as artisans or semi-skilled workers and twenty-one per cent as unskilled workers. Only a few of these managed to make their fortunes.

The strengthening and diffusion of anti-Jewish sentiment in the United States appear rather to be the result of interaction between the European substrata of the US population and the problems of a society in rapid and spectacular transformation. Wave after gigantic wave of immigrants made the country's ethnic composition and the problems associated with it ever more complex.

Anti-Jewish sentiment in the United States made a great leap forward with the Soviet Revolution. The intensity of this paroxysm was demonstrated in 1918 when the US government published *The German Bolshevik Conspiracy*, which contained documents that had been purchased at a very high price by a US diplomat in St Petersburg in the winter of 1917–18. The government endorsed these documents, even though it had no real proof of their authenticity. As it turned out, they were forgeries, created with the specific aim of discrediting the Bolsheviks through the use of anti-Jewish stereotypes. Their message was clear and simple: the Bolsheviks, and particularly Trotsky, were financed and directed by a "Rhinish-Westphalian syndicate" headed by Jewish bankers.

Once again the Jews were associated with an international conspiracy, and this time with ramifications in the United States: according to a magazine called *The Anti-Bolshevik*, the United States had entered the First World War in 1917 as a result of the secret machinations of the Jews.

These ravings were accepted as truth by, among others, Henry Ford, founder of the automobile factory and also, at the end of his life, the founder of one of the most important cultural institutions of the United States: the Ford Foundation. In November 1918 Ford acquired *The Dearborn Independent*, a weekly newspaper. On 22 May 1920, only two weeks after *The Times* article on *The Protocols*, *The Dearborn Independent* published the first of several articles denouncing the inordinate economic power of the Jews. From then on it was a crescendo: Ford's paper reiterated the conclusions drawn from *The Protocols of the Elders of Zion*: the Jews, led by a top-secret global directorate, wanted to rule the entire world.

The Dearborn Independent had a circulation of about 300,000 copies; Ford car salesmen collected subscriptions to the paper. All the anti-Semitic articles that appeared in it were reissued in a volume entitled *The International Jew*, which sold half a million copies and was translated into German, Russian, Spanish and thirteen other languages. Later an abridged version was used as part of Nazi propaganda; Hitler kept a photograph of Henry Ford on his desk, even after Ford abandoned his militant anti-Semitism. The publication of these articles was only part of Ford's anti-Semitic activity: he also hired detectives to find out who were the members and where was the meeting-place of the secret directorate of the Elders of Zion; and he sent a Russian émigré into Mongolia in search of the imaginary Hebrew original of *The Protocols*.

The "Reasons" for Henry Ford's Anti-Semitism

How did Ford explain his anti-Semitic convictions? In a 1921 interview he told a fantastic story: as he was travelling to Europe, in the hope of convincing the Europeans to end the First World War, two Jews approached him on board ship. According to Ford, they began to talk to him "of the power of the Jewish race and of how they controlled the world thanks to their control of the gold market: the Jew, and he alone, could end the war. I did not believe them, and I said so; they then entered into particulars and told me how the Jews were rich and controlled the press. In the end, they convinced me." And Ford, in his turn, convinced many other Americans of the "Jewish plot."

Left: this 1946 photograph shows Henry Ford with his wife in the first motor car, produced fifty years earlier.
Above: a print celebrating the emancipation of black Americans from slavery and encouraging them to enrol in the Union Army.

Democracy, however, produces its own antibodies, and protest grew in the United States. Religious figures, intellectuals and politicians denounced the anti-Semitic campaigns as false and dangerous. In 1928 Ford was sued by Jewish plaintiffs; in the same year General Motors overtook him in the automobile market, just as he was about to launch a new model in which he had invested all his company's capital. Ford withdrew the accusations against the Jews made in his publications and promised to withdraw all copies from circulation. But the anti-Semitic campaign had already had a political effect, in that it had been one cause of the passing of a series of restrictive immigration laws that culminated in the 1924 Johnson Bill, which set up a quota system favouring "Nordic" peoples over all others. As a result, the influx of Jews into the United States was drastically reduced.

The United States was to adhere to this strict quota system until its entry into the war (when immigration was actually reduced to about ten per cent of the quo-

Anti-Semitism contin-ued its sinister growth in the United States, home of the world's largest and most integrated Jewish community.

tas), despite the desperation of thousands fleeing Hitler. And so it was that a tradgedy like the St Louis incident could occur: in 1939 this ship, carrying more than 900 Jewish refugees from Hitler's Germany, was turned away from a US port. Eventually, the boat was forced to return to Europe, where many of its passengers died in the Holocaust.

At the height of the war, when news of Hitler's massacres was increasingly frequent, detailed and reliable, anti-Semitism continued its sinister growth in the United States, despite the fact that it was now the home of the world's largest and most integrated Jewish community. On 30 April 1943, a certain high official of the US government, who was involved in discussions with the British about what could be done to save at least some of the European Jews from extermination, noted in his diary that one had to be careful not to give credence to Hitler's accusations that the Americans were fighting "on behalf of our Jewish citizens, incited by them, and under their direction". He thought, with good reason, that such accusations could find an echo in part of American public opinion.

The ghost of *The Protocols* continued to haunt the United States while millions of Jews were being murdered in Nazi gas chambers, and even afterwards. In Alan Parker's *Mississippi Burning* (1988) — a fine film about racial integration in the southern United States in the 1960s — a leader of the Ku Klux Klan says that it is the duty of true Americans to fight against Communist and Jewish oppression... much as Henry Ford had maintained 40 years earlier.

Henry Ford was one of the principal architects of a "new world": that of the Taylorist-Fordist factory, of salary incentives linked to productivity, of mass car-ownership. Every "new world" creates fears, anxieties, misgivings. The past then seems an ideal, stable, comprehensible world in which relationships between people were founded in solidarity. This is true even for the protagonists of that "new world". Once again we see that anti-Semitism is not only a "residue of the past": it has also been characteristic of the individuals and social classes in the vanguard of modernity. And ironically, while in the West, an anti-Semite like Ford could fear communism as a Jewish plot, in the new Soviet Union, communists themselves did not avoid anti-Semitism.

Russian Bolsheviks do not Escape Prejudice

The Bolsheviks took power in Russia on 7 November 1917. Contemporary observers watched in amazement (whether in joy or despair) the birth of another "new world", one that had been heralded by the growth of a great socialist movement in Europe during the second half of the nineteenth century.

The following day, Vladimir Ilyich Ulyanov, known as Lenin, the leader of the victorious revolution, asked Trotsky to become Commissar of Internal Affairs. Trotsky, like Lenin, was a pseudonym; the revolutionary's real name was Lev Davidovich Bronstein, and he was Jewish. Trotsky felt that his new appointment was a mistake, as he described in his autobiography: "I opposed it; I even used the national argument — was it worth it to give my enemies the weapon of my Jewish origins as well?" A few years earlier one of the

Left: not even Trotsky, photographed here in exile in Paris in 1929, was immune from the discrimination that the Stalinist ruling elite practised against Jewish revolutionaries. Below: a Jewish tailor's workshop in New York at the beginning of the twentieth century.

directors of the largest Jewish socialist organization, the *Bund*, had asked Trotsky if he thought of himself primarily as a Russian or as a Jew. Trotsky responded drily, "Neither. You are mistaken. I am a social democrat, and that is all." This makes his later insistence on his Jewish origins as an obstacle to his appointment as Commissar for Internal Affairs all the more significant.

But anti-Jewish prejudice was not only widespread among those convinced of the existence of a Jewish-Communist plot. Ten years before the 1917 Revolution, a revolutionary newspaper printed a joke about the different strains of socialism among the Russian émigrés: "The Bolsheviks are a purely Russian faction, but the Mencheviks are a Jewish faction; so it wouldn't have been a bad idea for us Bolsheviks to have organized a pogrom in the Party." The joke, in itself coarse, was even more unpalatable in a Russia racked by frequent and terrible pogroms. Who had the bad taste to publish it in the socialist press? Joseph Vissarionovich Djugashvili, better known as Stalin, the future head of the Communist Party and supreme ruler of the Soviet Union.

The post-emancipation revival of anti-Jewish movements all over Europe, the political use of anti-Semitism among the masses, the rise of the Zionist movement, the political dislocation of a considerable portion of the Jewish intelligentsia, the low economic status of most Jews and the fact that many poor or proletarian Jews clung to the hope of a socialist

revolution, the foundation of Jewish workers' organizations: all these were elements that obliged the socialist movement to overcome the economic anti-Semitism of early socialism (which was still alive and well, as we have seen, at the beginning of the Dreyfus affair) and seriously reconsider the "Jewish question". In tandem with this came the failure of liberal emancipation and its logical consequence, assimilation — ideals which had long been cherished in much of socialist thought.

Religious Minority or Ethnic Minority?

The birth of the Zionist movement and the founding of autonomous non-Zionist Jewish workers' organizations both derived from the need to confront anti-Semitism and its political uses. Lenin — who had in theory essentially denied Jews the status of nationals — fought with particular bitterness against these Jewish workers' organizations. But socialist anti-Semitism was covert rather than overt. The slogan "anti-Semitism is the socialism of imbeciles" (erroneously attributed to the German social democratic leader August Bebel) expresses the attitude shared by socialist leaders in various countries, despite their different — and at one point opposing — strategic and political prospects. Not even Stalin could allow himself to express openly the anti-Semitic attitudes that he nevertheless tolerated and encouraged under the guise of anti-Zionism.

The importance of this universal denouncement of anti-Semitism by the organized labour movement cannot be underestimated. For the first time in history, organizations that were deeply rooted in the working classes rejected the hatred of the Jews, described it as reactionary, and promoted a counteroffensive. The character of that counteroffensive was predominantly pedagogical: it rested on the demonstration that the Jew was not an "alien" — he was one of us. This idea, however, was at odds with the fact that the Jew, once given the opportunity to become a citizen like any other, continued to be different. In many cases this was of his own volition: he wanted to be different and claimed the right to be so.

Left: a 1923 portrait of Lenin.
Below: the seat of the KGB in Moscow.
Above: a 1940s' portrait of Stalin.

The Zionist movement once founded, grew rapidly, and, although it was for a long time a minority affiliation, it soon became a potent presence in international politics.

The socialists, like the liberals, failed to see the importance of what we today perceive clearly as the heart of the matter. Anti-Jewish prejudice in its "modern" guise of anti-Semitism raised this issue, which Jean-Paul Sartre was to articulate after the Nazi genocide: there was (and is) no "Jewish question"; but there was (and is) an "anti-Semitic question". The problem, therefore, is not to understand if and in what ways the Jews are different from other people, but rather to understand the mental mechanism that triggers a hatred of the Jews that is quite independent of their historical character.

This, however, was not the intellectual ambit in which the socialist and liberal movements acted; thus the movement was unable to fathom the question of the Jewish presence in European society and, once in power, was unable to subdue the anti-Semitic feelings of the masses. Indeed, later socialist leaders exploited those feelings quite cynically under the pretext of a struggle against imaginary Zionist plots.

The inability of the socialists to identify the active proponents of anti-Jewish hatred and the causes of this persistent collective phobia led to a fundamental misconstruction: the "Jewish question" became focused on the victims, as if the reasons for the hatred to which they were subjected were really hidden somewhere within their common identity. Besides, the

facts seemed to support this notion: the Zionist movement was founded, grew, and soon became a potent presence in international politics, although it was for a long time a minority affiliation; meanwhile, a Jewish workers' movement developed with the aim of solving the problems of the numerous Jewish victims of the diaspora in the countries in which they lived.

The essential question, therefore, became whether the Jews were a religious minority or an ethnic minority. Such a question in itself runs the risk of reducing Jewish identity to a simple matter of religious preference, especially in Eastern Europe, where often — and not only in the case of the Jews — the two categories were not easily distinguishable.

However, the problem was not only theoretical: at the beginning of the twentieth century it became of immediate practical importance in vast multi-ethnic states, such as the dominions of the Tsar and the Austro-Hungarian Empire. In the West (as demonstrated, for example, in the writings of the German social democrat Karl Kautsky), the socialists supported the idea of assimilation, even though they had to admit that it was complicated and would take a long time.

In Austria, too, the socialists were convinced that assimilation would prevail in the end. For Otto Bauer, the leading theorist of the Austrian social democrats, in medieval times "the Jews were indisputably a

Below: Russian Jews waiting in line at Customs and Immigration, having just disembarked in the port of New York.

nation". Nevertheless, for Bauer the formula that Austrian socialists had applied to other nations — that of a national-cultural autonomy that can leave aside the question of territory — could not be applied to contemporary Jews. Despite Bauer's reservations, this formula seemed to be tailor-made for the Jews and was adopted by the largest Jewish socialist (non-Zionist) organizations, such as the Bund (the general union of Jewish workers in Poland, Lithuania and Russia).

A Problem for Revolutionary Russia

In the great Russian Empire the situation was particularly complicated: there was the considerable influence of the Bund, plus a strong Zionist movement with conspicuous socialist and Marxist elements.

Once in power, the Bolsheviks approached the problem of the various nationalities by applying the principle of self-determination. Each people had the right to choose its own political organization, and to decide whether or not it would become part of a multi-ethnic state. In the former Tsarist Empire, where dozens and dozens of different ethnic groups lived together, the principle of self-determination implied the possibility of secession, of separation. This possibility is obviously viable if each people has its own

territory. For the Bolsheviks, belonging to a specific territory was an essential component in the definition of a nation; and that was the missing element in the Jewish "nation", which was dispersed all over the world. Nevertheless, many Jews felt themselves "separate", and if the Jews were not a nation then at any rate they had national characteristics: common traditions and a common language. According to the Census of 1897, ninety-seven per cent of Russian Jews declared Yiddish (which Lenin

Far left: American Jews welcome their brothers and sisters from Europe with open arms.
Left: Rabbi with Torah by Marc Chagall.

dismissed with contempt as a kind of pidgin) to be their mother tongue.

How could the Jewish riddle be solved in revolutionary Russia? The Bolsheviks believed that the Jews could become a "nation" only if some of them took to agriculture (and this coincided with proposals made by the Bund): part of the Jewish population must become a social class with strong ties to the land, which could then provide the basis of a national market. Thus Stalin came to the same theoretical conclusions as the Zionist movement.

The practical results of these theoretical conclusions were, however, very different. The Zionist movement set in motion a flow of migrants, each of whom had made a free and informed choice to create a state in which he or she could contribute in freedom to a new chapter in Jewish history. In the Soviet case, by contrast, thousands upon thousands of Jews were transferred — more or less by force — to agricultural colonies, and an "autonomous region for the Jews" was set up in Birobistan in Central Asia. Historically rooted in the cities, the Jews felt at home neither in the countryside nor on the border of Manchuria. The project dreamed up by the Soviet government failed completely; but thereafter the authorities could refer to that failure as the Jewish "refusal" of a solution, thereby exonerating themselves from responsibility for the still-unresolved problems of the Jewish minority.

After the Revolution the struggle against anti-Semitism was fierce and open on the legal front as elsewhere, because (according to a decree of July 1918), "the anti-Semitic movement and the pogroms against the Jews [were] contrary to the interests of the workers' and peasants' Revolution". Then the situation changed: anti-Semitism was still formally prohibited, but it was in fact tolerated and even used to political ends. Trotsky observed with disdain that Stalin had not hesitated to use it against him.

Even so, there was no organized and widespread

"IT IS NOT THAT THE JEWS ARE DISLOYAL"

What follows is significant evidence of the persistence of anti-Jewish prejudice in Soviet life. Nahum Goldmann, who for many years was President of the Global Jewish Congress, recalls how he, as an observer of the Zionist movement at the Society of Nations, met Litvinov, then the Soviet Minister for Foreign Affairs.

One day Litvinov came to Geneva with a fourteen-member delegation, of whom eleven were Jews. I asked the Minister, "But why do you need a minjan?" [The Jewish term "minjan" means an assembly of

at least ten of the faithful.] Litvinov, who spoke Yiddish very well, laughed and said, "It's simple. I need them to speak French, English and German, and in Russia only the Jews speak foreign languages."

Many years later, in the mid-1960s, the Zionist leader, who remembered that conversation with Litvinov clearly, asked some experts to investigate the reasons for the total absence of Jews among Soviet diplomats. The research proved fruitless, so Goldmann went directly to Andrei Gromyko, the Soviet Minister for Foreign Affairs, and asked him to explain. Gromyko replied testily that it had nothing to do with anti-Semitism, adding: "The Jewish people are by their nature international, so we are cautious. It is not that the Jews are disloyal, only that they have too many friends, relatives and connections for our taste." ■

mass persecution (although many Jews were severely and unjustly persecuted), and there was no open legal discrimination.

Even before the Bolsheviks came to power, on 2 April 1917, the Russian Revolution had emancipated the Jews by repealing the 650 provisions of the law that discriminated against them. From thenceforth the Jews were, on paper, equal to all other citizens of the former Tsarist Empire. Many Jews moved up the social scale and the Soviet hierarchy. For many years, Stalin's closest collaborator was Lazar Moiseevich Kaganovich, who, as is clear from his patronymic, was Jewish.

In 1929 about 1.7 per cent of the Soviet population was Jewish, but about 2.9 per cent of those enrolled in the Soviet army were Jews. Of these, the proportion of Jewish officers is even greater (4.3 per cent) and among officers who played a political role, the proportion rises again (to 8.6 per cent). From 1930 to 1939, a Jew — Maxim Maximovich Litinov (originally Meir Wallach) — was in charge of Soviet foreign policy. He was, however, removed from office when in August 1939 the Soviet Union signed a non-aggression pact with Nazi Germany, known as the Molotov-Ribbentropp Pact.

Where blame was needed, Jews continued to be convenient scapegoats. Even in post-Soviet Russia there are organizations — such as the *Pamiat* (Memory) Society — that practise, under the transparent guise of anti-Zionism, a militant anti-Semitism.

The "Conspiracy of the White Shirts"

Anti-Zionism was the mask which disguised one anti-Jewish episode after another, both in the Soviet Union (which in 1947 voted in the UN in favour of the founding of the state of Israel) and in the countries that became Communist after 1945. A political position that was in itself legitimate (even many — perhaps most — Jews were at first averse to Zionist ideas) was transformed into an attitude tainted by anti-Semitism.

In 1947 the Soviet authorities banned a book (already in galley proofs) about the atrocities perpe-

Left: Litvinov, the Soviet Minister for Foreign Affairs, with his wife.

In post-Soviet Russia there are organizations — such as the Pamiat *(Memory) Society — that practise, under the transparent guise of an aversion to Zionism, a militant anti-Semitism.*

trated against the Jews by the Nazis. The team of researchers that had gathered information for the book was headed by two well-known Russian Jewish writers: Ilya Gregorievich Ehrenburg and Vasili Semionovich Grossman. The dossier was edited for the Jewish Anti-Fascist Commission of the Soviet Union, an organisation founded on 24 August 1941, a few weeks after the Nazi invasion of the Soviet Union. Composed of eminent Soviet Jewish personalities, during the war the Commission played an important political and propaganda role. After the war, however, its members were regarded with increasing suspicion and were accused of being "cosmopolitans".

The Commission was dissolved in November 1948, and afterwards its members were imprisoned. They were tried in 1952, just as the supremely-contrived "case" of the alleged "conspiracy of the white shirts" exploded. The Soviet secret police accused several eminent Jewish doctors of having hatched a "Zionist" plot to eliminate the most important leaders of the Communist Party. In the subsequent poisonous atmosphere, the members of the Jewish Anti-Fascist Commission were tried and condemned to death. This was followed by a wave of eliminations of Jewish intellectuals: more than 450 of them.

The idea that every Jew was complicit with "international Zionism" was frequently argued — as, for example, in the show trial of several leaders of the Czech Communist Party, among them Arthur London, author of *The Confession*, which was made into a film of the same name by Constantin Costa-Gavras in 1970. London's jailers even told him, "We will destroy you and all your filthy race! Hitler was what he was, but at least he killed Jews... Too many escaped from the gas chambers. But where Hitler failed, we will succeed!"

Unlike his less fortunate co-defendants, London was acquitted — French Communists intervened in his favour and managed to save his life. London, who had fought in the international brigades in the Spanish Civil War and with the French Resistance during World War II, went back to France; he remained a Communist, but in his telling account of Stalinist crimes, he denounced the unjust persecution of which he had been the victim, and the methods of Stalin and his acolytes as they operated behind the veil of "a struggle against the enemies of the people".

In the "new world" of "socialism in practice", the anti-Semitism that was condemned both in theory and in the law was never conquered in everyday life. In reality it was frequently used as a weapon in the political struggle. And with the transformation of Soviet democracy into dictatorship, the country lost the possibility, which free speech provides, of overcoming prejudice. But even in democracies, the paranoid climate of the Cold War continued to nurture anti-Semitism. In 1953 in the United States, Ethel and Julius Rosenberg were accused of spying for the Soviet Union and executed. Whether they were guilty or not, their Jewishness helped make them suspect. Again, the anti-Semitic idea that all Jews are by nature cosmopolitan and disloyal towards the nation in which they live held sway.

Left: the Russian writer Ilya Ehrenburg meets the French actor Yves Montand, who starred in the film The Confession, *in Moscow in 1963. Below: Jewish colonists working the land in Palestine after the Second World War.*

Chapter 6

THE TRAGEDY OF
THE HOLOCAUST

WITH THE RISE OF NAZISM AND ITS RACIST DOCTRINE, ANTI-SEMITISM UNDERGOES A CHILLING TRANSFORMATION. THE JEWS "DO NOT DESERVE TO LIVE". SIX MILLION ARE EXTERMINATED WITH EFFICIENT AND BUREAUCRATIC MACHINERY IN HITLER'S "FINAL SOLUTION".

The 30th January 1933: it is a date that humanity will never forget. On that day the President of the German Republic, Marshal Paul Ludwig von Beneckendorf und von Hindenberg, conferred the office of Chancellor upon Adolf Hitler. It was the beginning of a pitiless dictatorship that gave birth to a new state: the Third Reich. Within a few years, Germany and the entire world were plunged into the most extensive and destructive war in human history. By the end of that war, according to the most reliable sources, there were over 51 million dead, 45.5 per cent of whom were civilians.

Hitler was the absolute leader — the Führer — of the NSDAP, the *Nationalsozialistische Deutsche Arbeiter Partei* (The National Socialist Party of German Workers); the party was formed in 1920 out of an earlier political group that had arisen in the period immediately after the First World War. Like the Italian Fascist Party, it practised violence systematically as a means of political struggle and had a strong paramilitary wing made up of ex-combatants.

In the serious economic, political and moral crises that rocked Germany in the late 1920s, the National Socialists (Nazis for short) gained an extraordinary electoral ascendancy. Between May 1928 and November 1932, Germans went to the polls four times. At the end of May 1928, the NSDAP won 2.6 per cent of the vote; a little over two years later, in September 1930, they polled 18.3 per cent; in July 1932, in another extraordi-

Left: a member of the SA poses in front of a Jewish-owned shop in Berlin in 1933; the sign reads "Germans! Defend yourselves! Do not buy from Jews!".

For Rosenberg, human history was characterized by the permanent tension between the values of the 'Northerners' (he seems to have preferred this to the term 'Aryans') and the lack of values in 'racial confusion'.

nary leap, 37.4 per cent of the electorate voted for Hitler's party. The German political situation was muddled and potentially explosive, but the results of yet another election in November 1932 showed that the Nazis were maintaining their position: one in three continued to vote for the NSDAP, which made it the majority party.

Hitler's rise to power thus seemed to have the official blessings of the legal democratic process, but in reality this was not the case. The Nazis — with the complicity of powerful interest groups — had intimidated, beaten and killed their adversaries. Moreover, the NSDAP had abundant resources at their disposal, more than any other political group. These funds had been supplied by the most powerful sectors of Germany society — industry, finance, the military and agriculture — in order to combat Communism. This, however, is not enough to explain the large consensus won by the Nazis before they came to power.

The Racist Doctrine of Nazism

Hitler's message to a profoundly frustrated and disorientated Germany was one of national redemption. According to the Führer, Germany could recover only by fighting against the tendency — characteristic of the modern era and the decline of civilization — towards the mixing together of the races. He maintained that this was a violation of the "fundamental laws" of nature: "a law that is fundamental and almost inviolable... each animal mates with a member of its own species." Racial interbreeding was therefore a sin; in fact, "the sin against blood and race is the original sin of this world and marks the end of the people that commit it". It was therefore necessary to reverse that tendency and create a state that was "jealously vigilant, in order to conserve the best elements of its own race". Hitler prophesied that such a state "must one day become the ruler of the world". Thus reads the penultimate phrase of the bible of National Socialism: *Mein Kampf* (*My Struggle*), the two-volume work written by Hitler in 1924. The German or "Aryan" was obviously the "race" to be preserved.

Another work essential to Nazi ideology appeared in 1930: Alfred Rosenberg's *Der Mythus des XX Jahrun-*

derts (*The Myth of the Twentieth Century*). Hitler considered it too abstruse, perhaps more appropriate to an educated readership, or one that considered itself to be so. The book was dominated by one fundamental theme: race and purity of blood. For Rosenberg, human history was characterized by permanent tension between the values of the "Northerners" (he seems to have preferred this to the term "Aryans") and the lack of values in "racial confusion". The Church was and continued to be among those responsible for this "confusion", having preached a "universalism without limits"; "humanitarian harangues" and the theory of equality among men had caused incalculable damage to civilization. It was necessary to preserve, purify and improve the "Northern" race. The voters who went over to the NSDAP responded positively to this message, the keystone of which was the most virulent racism and anti-Semitism. Many Germans accepted the idea that the principle cause of their problems was other "races", and in particular the Jews. Less than forty years after the success of the Anti-Semitic Party in 1893, German anti-Semitism had reached very different heights.

What were the origins of the Nazi doctrine of racism? In the vast sea of German anti-Semitism, Hitler seems to have been influenced most profoundly by a "minor" source. Apparently in his youth he read the racist review *Ostara*, whose editor-in-chief proposed the creation of an order of male Aryan heroes, destined to be the *avant-garde* of the blonde, blue-eyed ruling race in the bloody battle with inferior races. Even more thoroughly despised than a member of an inferior race was the half-breed, the result of the mixing of the races. The product of miscegenation is indelibly marked, but so too is anyone who practises it, particularly (could it be otherwise?) the woman.

Below: the yellow star that Jews were obliged to wear upon their clothing in Nazi Germany.

A PROBLEM FOR THE NAZIS: WHO IS JEWISH?

The passage from anti-Semitic theory to practice posed a problem for the Nazis (and later for the Italian Fascists and all the satellite countries of the German Reich), and learned experts of the regime dedicated themselves to finding a solution. It was easy to say that the Jews must be expelled from public administration and schools, or that their property must be "Aryanized". It was far more difficult and complicated, however, to identify the individuals to be persecuted. Despite all the theoretical work and "scientific research" on race that had been done in Germany, and later in Italy, criteria other than religious affiliation could not be found.

A decree of 7 April 1933 announced the dismissal from public administration of all functionaries who "were not of Aryan descent". But who was "not of Aryan descent"? The reply came a few days later: anyone who had one or more Jews among his or her parents or grandparents. Another question then arose: how was one to know if the

father, mother, grandfather or grandmother was a Jew? The answer was easy: they were Jews if they practised Judaism. The definition was thus not in fact based upon racial criteria but on religious affiliation. The criterion adopted in 1933 still begged many questions. On the basis of it, anyone who had

even only one-quarter of "Jewish blood" was added to those who were considered "pure" Jews. It follows that the Jewish quarter prevailed over three-quarters of "Aryan blood". Thus an entire section of German society was abandoned as "Jewish".

After the Nuremberg laws (September 1935), the learned experts of the regime decreed that in Germany there were not only "Aryans" and "non-Aryans" but also a kind of "third race", the *mischlinge*, those "crossed with Jews", who were not themselves Jews but rather "part-Jewish".

The Germans, then, were divided into three groups. First there were the "Aryans". Then there were the "Jews", a group including all those who had at least

three Jewish grandparents, plus those who had two Jewish grandparents and furthermore were either practising Jews on 15 September 1935; or on the same date were married or engaged to a Jewish man or woman (classified as acts of "philojudaism"); or were born of a marriage contracted before 15 September 1935 in which one of the two parents was either of "pure" Jewish descent or three-quarters Jewish; or were illegitimate and born after 3 July 1936 of parents one of whom was of "pure" Jewish descent or three-quarters Jewish. To determine whether or not grandparents or parents were Jewish it was necessary, once again, to fall back on the criterion of religious affiliation. Finally there was the "third race", the *mischlinge*. Those "crossed with Jews" were divided into two subcategories: the "first-class *mischlinge*" were those who had two Jewish grandparents but on 15 September 1935 did not themselves belong to the Jewish faith, or on the same date were not married to Jews; the "second-class *mischlinge*" were those who had only one Jewish grandparent. First-class *mischlinge* were subjected to more severe discrimination than those of the second class. It is important to note that, under the pseudoscientific criteria of Nazi anti-Semitic racism, siblings — or even twins — could be put into different categories, one as a Jew, the other as a "first-class *mischlinge*", if the former was in love with a Jew and the latter was not. ■

The concept of "racial confusion" employed by Rosenberg was derived from Houston Stewart Chamberlain, Richard Wagner's son-in-law, an Englishman who became a German citizen in 1917 when, at the height of the First World War, he thought that Germany would win. Chamberlain — together with the positivist Karl Eugen Dühring (1833–1921) and the Orientalist Paul de Lagarde (pseudonym of Paul Anton Böttincher, 1827–91) — was the third person in the trinity of German "classics" of anti-Semitism. His principle work, *Die Grundlagen des XIX Jahrunderts* (*The Foundations of the Nineteenth Century*), was published in 1899 in two volumes of about 1,550 pages. A kind of "racist bible", it had immediate success and gained the approval of a surprisingly wide range of people: Theodore Roosevelt, President of the United States; writers with socialist and humanitarian sympathies, such as George Bernard Shaw and Leo Tolstoy; and the German Emperor Wilhelm II, whose enthusiasm for Chamberlain's works was such that he ordered them to be assigned as compulsory reading in Prussian teacher-training courses.

Chamberlain had taken up the basic ideas of Gobineau, for whom race was the driving force of history. His main concern was the need to preserve Germanic

Top left: Alfred Rosenberg with Hitler in 1938. Bottom left: the winner of a competition for "Nordic heads" in Nazi Germany. Below: the window of a Berlin shop in 1933, displaying an instrument for measuring the differences of dimension between Aryan and non-Aryan crania.

blood from being adulterated by extraneous elements. What did "race" mean to Chamberlain? In order to identify it, he used obvious physical characteristics (hair colour, eye colour, and the configuration of the face) and also anthropometric factors (the form of the cranium and the length of the nose), which were favoured by the crude biologists of positivism. In addition he claimed that the true criterion for recognizing a race was of a psychological nature, because the signs of race were inscribed above all in the moral order.

However, when Chamberlain asked himself how, in practical terms, the German race could be preserved from admixture, he inevitably resorted to biological criteria, since the race was made up of flesh-and-blood individuals who had been born of parents and had reproduced in their turn.

Paul de Lagarde also claimed that "Germanism does not reside in the blood but in the spirit", but nevertheless put his readers on guard against miscegenation. Something analogous took place in 1938 when the Italian Fascists adopted anti-Semitic laws: the Mussolini regime defined its anti-Semitism as "of the spirit", but in order to identify the objects of persecution it had to use biological criteria.

Here we see how concepts that were originally developed in descriptive studies of the classification of living beings ("race" as a group of individuals of a single species who are distinguished from other groups in the same species by one or more constant and transmissible external physical characteristics) are then transferred to the psychological and moral order. This unjustified and scientifically-groundless shift of meaning — in a concept that was developed for specific fields of enquiry and then applied elsewhere — did not take place in a void: it happened in an age of imperialist expansion, with its corollary ideas of the superiority of the colonists over the colonized. It was developed and adopted by people who jumped from the idea of a nation to nationalism, in which one's own nation is superior to all others. It was the necessary result of a mental and political attitude that was both mystical and irrational.

Left: this painting by Wolfgang Willrich represents the ideal German family of the Nazi period in a bucolic setting outside their home.
Below: visitors to an exhibition during the Hitler regime look at charts illustrating the physiognomic characteristics of the different "races".

The Anti-Semitic Crusade as Religious Duty

In order to take root, racism and anti-Semitism needed a hierarchical vision of humanity based on confused prejudices rather than on rational evidence. Race, therefore, could only be defined — and preserved — by means of biological criteria. It is not surprising, then, that racists and Nazis often had recourse to images and examples from animal husbandry. The tragic official doctrine of the Third Reich could thus, with reason, be stamped as "veterinary rigmarole".

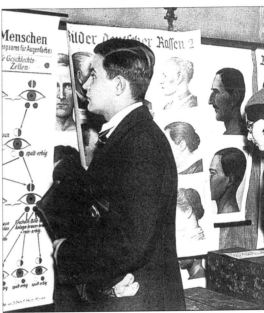

In *Mein Kampf*, Hitler poses a rhetorical question: "Is there any filth, any infamy, especially in social life, in which no Jew was involved?" The answer, for the *Führer*, was clearly negative: "Jews act like the worst bacilli; they poison souls". Their tools were the press, the arts, literature and cinema. Chamberlain claimed that even the march of science had been tainted by the "Jewish" spirit. During the Nazi regime his followers included illustrious and servile academics in search of easy fame and political advantage.

The Jew's essential weapon, declared the Führer, was "the Jewish theory of Marxism", which proclaimed equality, contested the importance of race, and was therefore contrary to "external nature". If it triumphed "it would bring the end of every humanly compatible order", and so, Hitler affirmed, "defending myself from

the Jews, I fight to defend the work of the Lord" (albeit a very different Lord from the one who usually comes to mind when that name is invoked). Chamberlain devoted a hundred pages to proving that Christ was not a Jew. Rosenberg claimed that, in order to overcome definitively the ancient attempt to Jewify the Germans, it was necessary "to eliminate once and for all the so-called Old Testament as a religious text" (even though it was an integral part of Christian belief).

The racist anti-Semitic crusade was thus for Hitler and the Nazis a religious duty. At the same time, it was a duty of national "self-defence". The German dictator adopted the vision of *The Protocols*: the Jews sought to impose their dominance upon the world. In this they were helped (raved Hitler) by the French, who as a people were "sinking ever closer to the level of Negroes" and "cunningly, and with the support of the Jews in the interests of their goal of universal dominance" were endangering "the existence of the white race in Europe". They were also in cahoots with the Negro, "a being who is in his origins half monkey". If the Negro was half-animal, the Jew was the quintessence of cunning. For this reason, it is possible to say that in Hitler's thinking, if the Jew was the enemy, the black was truly the inferior (though of course anyone who was non-German was inferior in his scheme of things).

The Jew was the enemy because he was the bearer of the greater risk of racial contamination. He lived among the "Aryans", barely recognizable by the physical stigmata of the "typical Jew". Without a country, deprived of his own "living space", he could not participate in the universal struggle for power among "races" and peoples by the usual means of war for territorial conquest, for the expansion of his "living space". He must therefore use secret and immoral means, just like the popular image of the devil: astute, dishonest, corrupting, always ready to lure women, in particular, from the straight path. In *Mein Kampf* we read that "for hours the young black-haired Jew watches, his face illuminated by a Satanic joy, the girl who is unaware of her danger... As he systematically corrupts girls and women, he is not afraid to break down many of the barriers that blood has placed between him and other peoples."

The "barrier of blood" defined the Jew in a different way to that used in medieval and modern Europe. To be Jewish was no longer the consequence of a religious affiliation (Judaism) but rather of racial characteristics (Jewishness). According to Hannah Arendt, Jews "had always been able to save themselves from Judaism by means of conversion; from Jewishness there was no means of escape."

A Minority Faithful to the Nation's Values

On 30 January 1933, then, with the active support of a considerable portion of the German electorate a man and a party came to power with a vision and political programme to which anti-Semitism and racism were central. Few at that time, in Germany or elsewhere, guessed how the Nazis' anti-Semitic obsession would end; in 1933, it was not possible to foresee the horrors of the "final solution". Hitler had "only" said that he wanted a Germany that was *judenfrei*, free of Jews.

It was "only" a matter of ridding the nation of 525,000 German Jews, who were traditionally concentrated in the cities. As in other Jewish communities in Western Europe, among the German Jews there was a strong urge to assimilate. From 1900 onwards there were over 400 conversions each year, and twelve per cent of Jews married gentiles. About one in three Jews were white-collar workers, and seventeen per cent were blue-collar workers. Many Jews worked in commerce and the professions, but their importance in these sectors was nowhere near that attributed to them by anti-Semitic propaganda.

Still, the Jewish minority was a credit to the nation: we need only think of such names as Heinrich Heine, Karl Marx and Albert Einstein. Of the forty-four Germans who had won the Nobel Prize before Hitler came to power, eight were Jews (and a further four were of mixed Jewish and gentile origins). It was also a minority with a strong sense of loyalty to

Left: a scene from the film Suss the Jew, *made by order of the Nazi Minister for Propaganda, Joseph Goebbels; the film had the declared intention of instilling hatred for Jews in the German population.*
Below: the physicist Albert Einstein, author of the theory of relativity and winner of the Nobel Prize for physics in 1921; Jewish and originally of German nationality, Einstein became a US citizen.

DEUTSCHES-REICH

J

ISEPASS

Nr.

NAME DES PASSINHABERS

the German nation. During the First World War, 100,000 Jews had fought in the German armed forces and 12,000 had been killed in action. Nevertheless, in Germany as in other nations where Jews had participated *en masse* in the mobilization for war, they were accused of shirking their duties to the nation and of speculating in goods that were basic necessities. But German Jews were so attached to the customs and mentality of their country that Jews of other nationalities, when speaking of them, often quoted a proverbial Jewish quip: "Each country has the Jews it deserves."

In August 1933, Fritz Rosenfelder — the Jewish manager of a sports club in the small city of Württenberg — committed suicide. In his suicide note he wrote, "A German Jew cannot go on living, when he knows that the movement towards which Germany looks for its salvation considers him a traitor." A newspaper commented: "Fritz Rosenfelder was a reasonable man and he hanged himself! We are glad, and we see no reason why his fellow Jews should not take their leave of us in the same manner." Nine years earlier, a Jewish Italian intellectual, Felice Momigliano, had committed suicide for personal reasons. One of the most representative figures of the Italian Catholic community, Father Agostino Gemelli, founder and Rector of the Catholic University of the Sacred Heart in Milan and later President of the Pontifical Academy of Sciences, found nothing better to say in the review *Vita e pensiero* (*Life and Thought*) than:

"Would not the world be a better place if, together with positivism, socialism, free thought and Momigliano, all the Jews who continue the work of those who crucified Our Lord were to die as well? It would be a liberation."

These two comments, made in such different cultural contexts, demonstrate the continuity between Christian anti-Jewish sentiment and anti-Semitism. Both employ the same kind of language, with a view to exciting the same kind of emotions. In both cases, suicide — violence against oneself — is exalted as the means of ridding the speaker, and the world, of Jews. This reveals how both "traditional" anti-Jewish sentiment and "modern" anti-Semitism contain a germ of violence against the "Christ-killer" or the contaminator of racial purity.

For Hitler, the Germany of the Third Reich had to be *judenfrei*, free of Jews. From the beginning, this objective was pursued with laws that made the lives of German Jews ever more difficult and finally impossible. Perhaps in the beginning the Nazi regime did not intend to do what they subsequently went on to do, that is to exterminate the Jews. Nevertheless, violence was used extensively against Jews in a myriad of episodes — some well-known, others less so — both in the course of the Nazi struggle for power and after Hitler became

For Hitler, the Germany of the Third Reich had to be judenfrei, *free of Jews. From the beginning, this objective was pursued with laws that made the lives of German Jews ever more difficult and, finally, impossible.*

leader of the nation. Furthermore, the physical elimination of the Jews was contemplated as a real possibility in the anti-Semitic ideology of Nazism. As we have seen, in *Mein Kampf* Hitler wrote that the Jews "act like the worst bacilli". In June 1935 the bulletin of the Order of German Physicians compared the Jew to Koch's bacillus, the carrier of tuberculosis.

"The Solution Cannot Avoid Being Bloody"

The problem of the Jewish "bacillus" that was infecting the healthy body of the "Aryan race" could not be solved without bloodshed. The Nazis admitted this openly. In July 1933, Paul Joseph Goebbels — who was in charge of NSDAP propaganda from 1928 and Reich Minister for Information and Propaganda from 1933 to 1945 — stated in conversation with an English journalist: "Death to the Jews! For fourteen years, this has been our war cry. May they all drop dead."

A little more than three years later, in September 1936, Goebbels's viewpoint was endorsed by another leading Nazi, Julius Streicher, *Gauleiter* of Franconia. (Later, after the passing of the anti-Semitic laws of Nuremberg, 100,000 children in Franconia were made to swear "eternal enmity" to the Jews.) He was the editor of an anti-Semitic paper called *Der Strümer*, and was eventually condemned to death by the Nuremberg tribunal. Streicher's opinion was that: "It is an error to suppose that the Jewish problem can be solved without bloodshed: the solution cannot avoid being bloody."

As the state became more and more totalitarian, with every right emanating from the Führer and every citizen reduced to a subject, the Jews were systematically exposed to the fury of anti-Semitism. The campaign of hatred and violence was aimed not only at the Jews themselves but also at anything that was seen as "Jewish", from democracy to some of the most extraordinary achievements of modern science — such as psychoanalysis and the theory of relativity, products of the genius of two Jews, Sigmund Freud and Albert Einstein. Bonfires of books by Jewish and anti-Nazi authors were burned in the squares of many German cities. At the same time, German Jews were gradually being denied their rights. They began to emigrate: 25,000 Jews left Germany in the first half of 1933, and a further 50,000 emigrated between July of that year and September 1935. But not all had the chance to emigrate, and few countries were disposed to welcome them as immigrants.

In order to make Germany *judenfrei*, it was necessary to make life for Jews in the Reich ever more difficult. This was achieved with the Nuremberg laws of 15 September 1935: from that point onwards, Jews were not citizens of Germany and could not marry "Aryans". The Nuremberg laws were followed by a barrage of regulations that made it impossible for Jews to engage in many economic activities and most jobs and professions. But this was not enough: the Nazi leaders also thought it necessary constantly to exacerbate the "Aryan" anger against the Jews.

An occasion was offered when a young Jew, the son of deportees, assassinated a German diplomat in Paris. Three days later, on the night of 9 November 1938, anti-Semitic violence exploded. It became known as Kristallnacht, the night of broken glass, because of the attacks upon Jewish shops. One hundred and nineteen synagogues were burned down; 7,500 Jewish-owned shops were sacked; ninety-one Jews were killed and 26,000 were imprisoned in concentration camps. Kristallnacht was Goebbels's idea: he authorized the NSDAP and the Party militia to incite violent attacks. As in many explosions of anti-Semitic fury, the order came from above. This presented a turning-point in the

Left: a Jewish proprietor about to sweep the broken glass from the pavement in front of his Berlin shop on the morning of 10 November 1938. The glass had been broken by Nazi squads during the night. What happened that night, known as Kristallnacht, was an all-out pogrom, initiated by the regime in reaction to the assassination of a German diplomat in Paris. The results were, to say the least, appalling. On Hitler's explicit orders, those responsible were not prosecuted by the judicial authorities. Below: after the passing of the race laws by the Italian Fascist regime in 1938, the owner of a Roman shop puts a sign in the window to "reassure" customers (the sign reads "This shop is Aryan").

THE NAZI PROGRAMME AND THE REALIZATION

CHRONOLOGY

1933
30 January: Hitler is appointed Chancellor. **9 March:** Anti-Semitic attacks by the SA or *Sturmabteilungen* (storm troops) and the *Stahlheim* (steel helmets). **13 March:** Jewish shops are sacked in Braunschweig in Lower Saxony, in Beslavia on the River Oder; Jewish lawyers and judges are expelled from the tribunals. **March:** At Dachau the first concentration camp is constructed for political dissidents. **1 April:** The NSDAP proclaimed this a day of boycott of Jewish goods and services. **7 April:** A law is passed redefining the criteria for admission to the civil service; Jews are now forbidden to work in public administration. This is followed by provisions limiting the access of Jews to university education and some professions (such as the law). **21 April:** A law is passed forbidding the ritual slaughter of livestock for kosher meat. **10 May:** Books by Jewish authors and anti-Nazi writers are publicly burned in Berlin and other cities. **22 June – 5 July:** All political parties in Germany other than the Nazi Party are dissolved. **14 July:** The NSDAP is proclaimed the only legal political party. **October:** All the hospitals in Berlin are declared *frei* (free) of Jewish doctors (those expelled cannot be employed by other hospitals).

1934
2 August: Following the death of Hindenberg, Hitler also assumes the responsibility of Head of State.

1935
16 March: Conscription is introduced. **31 May:** Jews are declared unfit for military service. **15 September:** The Nuremberg laws are passed; afterwards, 100,000 children in Franconia swear "eternal enmity" for the Jews. In the months and years that follow, 13 executive orders are issued to accomplish the systematic exclusion of Jews from the state community. Work opportunities become restricted to an ever more limited number of jobs.

1936
3 March: Jewish doctors are forbidden to work in public hospitals.

1937
July: Buchenwald concentration camp is constructed.

1938
12–13 March: Annexation of Austria; 125,000 Austrian Jews are subjected to Nazi law. **9 June:** Destruction of the synagogue in Monaco. **1 August:** The Centre for Jewish Emigration is established in Vienna under the directorship of Adolf Eichmann. **25 July:** The professional qualifications of Jewish doctors are cancelled. **10 August:** Destruction of the synagogue at Nuremberg. **17 August:** An order is issued that, from 1 January 1939, Jews can only go by the first names recorded in a special list kept at the Reich Ministry of Internal Affairs; any Jew whose first name is not on the list must take the additional Jewish name of Sara (for a female) or Israel (for a male). **27 September:** Jews can no longer work in the law courts. **5 October:** The passports of German Jews are declared invalid. **6 November:** Herschel Grynszpan, the son of Jewish deportees, assassinates a secretary from the German Embassy in Paris. **9 November:** Using the Paris assassination as an excuse, a wave of anti-Semitic violence sweeps Germany in what becomes known as *Kristallnacht*: 119 synagogues are burnt down, 7,500 Jewish-owned shops are sacked, 91 Jews are killed and 26,000 are taken to concentration camps. **12 November:** The Jewish victims of *Kristallnacht* are ordered to pay pecuniary sanctions amounting to a billion marks as an "indemnity" to their persecutors. On the same day other orders are issued: the "regulation on the restoration of urban order by Jewish commercial enterprises", whereby Jews are obliged to pay back indemnities received from insurance companies of the Reich; the "regulation on the exclusion of Jews from German economic life", as a result of which Jewish properties are sold at ridiculously low prices; and the "order of the President of the Reich Chamber of Culture on the participation of Jews in public demonstrations", in which Jews are prohibited from entering cultural institutions such as museums and theatres. **15 November:** Jewish children and youths are excluded from all the schools of the Reich.

1939
24 January: Reinhard Heydrich establishes the Centre for

OF THE GENOCIDE OF THE JEWS

Jewish Emigration in Berlin, modelled on the one in Vienna. **1 September:** Two thousand seven hundred German tanks cross the border into Poland; the Second World War begins.

THE FIGURES OF GENOCIDE

How many Jews were exterminated in the anti-Semitic fury of the Nazis and their European allies, from the Italian Fascists to the collaborationist Vichy regime in France? Perhaps the exact figures will never be known. An encyclopaedic study of Jewish history, published in France in 1992 and edited by Eli Barnavi, proposed the figure of 5,948,500. This is close to six million, the death toll fixed in the collective memory; the figure was originally quoted in the testimony of a high official in the Reich's security service who attributed it to Adolf Eichmann. Eichmann declared that he would jump for joy in his grave if the number of Jews exterminated was five million, and this figure was confirmed in 1961 when he was tried in Israel and condemned to death. In his seminal reference book on the genocide — *The Destruction of the European Jews* — Raul Hilberg, who has been researching the question for thirty years, proposes 5,100,000 as a figure closer to the truth. He divides the victims by country as follows:

Poland	up to 3,000,000
USSR	over 700,000
Romania	270,000
Czechoslovakia	260,000
Hungary	over 180,000
Lithuania	up to 130,000
Germany	over 120,000
Netherlands	over 100,000
France	75,000
Latvia	70,000
Yugoslavia	60,000
Greece	60,000
Austria	over 50,000
Belgium	24,000
Italy (including Rhodes)	9,000
Estonia	2,000
Norway	less than 1,000
Luxembourg	less than 1,000
Danzig	less than 1,000

This amounts to over 5,000,000 victims, of whom 800,000 died during the construction of the ghettos and of starvation, 1,300,000 were killed in the so-called "mobile extermination operations" (such as mass shootings), and up to 3,000,000 disappeared in the Nazi extermination camps (1,000,000 in Auschwitz alone). A substantial number (2,700,000) were killed in 1942, the year of Hitler's greatest expansion. These figures, in themselves frightening, become almost inconceivable when considered in relation to the size of the Jewish population. In the so-called "Wannsee Protocol" the Nazis estimated the Jewish population of Europe to be over eleven million people. But they proposed to exterminate more because "The estimate of the number of Jews in various foreign countries... includes only practising Jews, since we have not yet a complete definition of what is a Jew according to racial criteria." The Jews who were exterminated account for about fifty per cent of the Jewish population as estimated in that document. Some communities disappeared altogether. The most striking case is that of Poland: of the 3,350,000 Polish Jews, 3,000,000 were exterminated, that is to say 89.5 per cent.

A *photograph of Reinhard Heydrich.*

Kristallnacht was followed by heavy restrictions on the Jews: they were excluded from the few economic activities that had hitherto remained open to them, barred from schools, from participating in public demonstrations, and from libraries, cinemas, museums, and theatres.

regime's anti-Semitic campaign: the implicit acknowledgement that the "Jewish problem" could not be solved without violence.

Nazis loudly proclaimed that the Jews themselves were really responsible for what had happened, not only because of the assassination but above all because their presence provoked the best and deepest sentiments of the German people. They had to pay for this. Burning, sacking, killing and deportation were not enough; the Germans must be compensated by the Jews. Thus the Jews would be hit where, according to the anti-Semites, it hurt them most: in their wallets. The underlying message of this absurd logic is clear: anything is permitted against the Jews while they continue to exist among us. It is therefore not surprising that *Kristallnacht* was followed by heavy restrictions on the Jews: they were excluded from the few economic activities that had hitherto remained open to them, barred from schools, from participating in public demonstrations, and from libraries, cinemas, museums and theatres.

The Fascist Race Laws

Europe in the 1930s was teaming with authoritarian regimes and dictatorships of the right, with the excep-

tion of the Soviet Union. The "mother" of right-wing European dictatorships was that of Fascist Italy. With a few exceptions on the fringe, Italian Fascism was not anti-Semitic. It is no accident that many Italian Jews were adherents of Fascism, because of their social position but often also because of their nationalist convictions.

In the second half of 1938 the Italian Fascist regime radically changed its position, but not without considerable internal strife. According to the minutes of the 6–7 October 1938 meeting of the Great Council of Fascism, the central organ of the regime, the "question of race" arose in Italy on the day of the proclamation of the Empire that followed the occupation of Ethiopia in 1936: "After the conquest of the Empire, [The Great Council of Fascism] declares the urgency of racial problems and the necessity of developing racial awareness... The Jewish problem is nothing but the metropolitan side of a general problem." Within a very short time an integrated minority became the object of discrimination and persecution, and its members became second-class citizens: mixed marriages were forbidden, Jews were denied access to schools and professions, and their right to own property was severely limited.

Left: Auschwitz extermination camp. Above: the covers of two issues of the Italian anti-Semitic monthly La difesa della razza *(The Defence of the Race).*

Right: a Fascist poster of 1938 showing the various things that were forbidden to Italian citizens of the Jewish religion. The poster reads: "There can be no Jews... in military and civil administrations... in the Fascist Party... in provincial and municipal institutions... in state institutions... in banks... in insurance companies. Jews are excluded from Italian schools."
Far right: Marshall Pétain, head of the Vichy Republic in Nazi-occupied France.

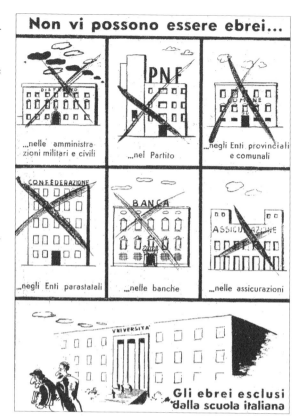

How did the Italian people react? Even considering that a dictatorial regime was in force, the ease with which the majority accepted the "politics of race" is chilling. Many elements contributed to this, but first and foremost was the effect of the anti-Jewish stereotypes that had been inculcated for centuries by the religious instruction of the Catholic Church, which had always seen the Jewish people as "Christ-killers". The ceremonies of Holy Week began with the injunction "*Oremus pro perfidis judeis*" ("Let us pray for the perfidious Jews").

Nevertheless, unlike in many other European countries, when the threat of massacre for Italian Jews loomed large after the Nazi occupation of the peninsula on 8 September 1943, many Italians — people without any particular religious or political commitment, as well as members of the Catholic clergy — helped Jews hide and escape deportation. This demonstrates all the

FRENCH JEWS UNDER FIRE

In 1940 the most complicated political situation and the most important Jewish community in the West were to be found in France. The French Jewish community at that point was between 300,000 and 350,000 strong, and about half its members — immigrants from Germany and the east — did not have French citizenship. After the fall of France in June 1940 the country was divided in two: to the north and west was the zone occupied by the Germans; in the south-east the French maintained their own sovereignty, however limited. The "collaborationist" government of this half-country was based in Vichy. The Head of State was Marshall Philippe Pétain, who had been Supreme Commander of the army from 1917–18 and was therefore a hero of the Great War. The Prime Minister was Pierre Laval. The part of France administered by Vichy was not an occupied country like Poland or Holland, but neither was it an independent state. Its status was ambiguous and difficult to define. In October 1940, the Vichy government opened an anti-Jewish campaign with a statute on Jews and a law on foreigners of the Jewish race, thereby pursuing its own autonomous political agenda. Jews were excluded from schools, public administration, and the liberal professions. Their assets were "Aryanized", that is to say appropriated. Jewish foreigners were imprisoned in concentration camps.

When the Nazis definitively decided upon the "final solution", the Vichy government at first resisted German requests for the

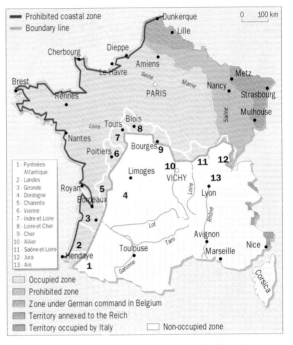

Map legend:
- Prohibited coastal zone
- Boundary line

1 - Pyrénées-Atlantique
2 - Landes
3 - Gironde
4 - Dordogne
5 - Charente
6 - Vienne
7 - Indre-et-Loire
8 - Loire-et-Cher
9 - Cher
10 - Allier
11 - Saône-et-Loire
12 - Jura
13 - Ain

- Occupied zone
- Prohibited zone
- Zone under German command in Belgium
- Territory annexed to the Reich
- Territory occupied by Italy
- Non-occupied zone

deportation of Jews. Then, in exchange for the promise of independence for the French police in the occupied zone (more a matter of appearance than reality), the Vichy government agreed to the deportation of Jews of "no nation" who had been interned in camps in the Vichy-controlled area for at least 18 months. This was the beginning of the road to Calvary for Jews who had sought refuge in France, and later for French Jews. Seventy-five thousand — between 21 and 25 per cent of the total — were massacred. Thus by the end of the war one Jew in every four or five of the pre-war Jewish population living on French soil was missing. That many escaped persecution

was due to the efforts of members of the Resistance, both Jews and non-Jews, who constructed a vast rescue network, especially for children. Others managed to escape from death with the help of compassionate individuals working on their own initiative. ■

more clearly the extent to which the Fascist regime was responsible for the fate of Italian Jews. They were hunted down with the assistance of a 1938 Census taken after the passing of the Italian race laws. Persecution was carried out with the help of the institutions of the Italian Social Republic — effectively a German satellite state founded by Mussolini in September 1943.

One element has been frequently overlooked in discussions of the Italian Fascist regime's switch to anti-Semitism: the international situation. Despite the dispositions drawn up during peace negotiations, which obliged the signatory nations to respect the rights of all their citizens, by 1938 many countries had anti-Jewish legislation. Nazi anti-Semitic laws came into force in

Austria after it was annexed to the German Reich in March 1938. But there were also anti-Jewish laws operating in Poland, Hungary, Bulgaria, Slovakia and Romania. In Poland, home of one of the largest Jewish communities in the world, Jews were excluded from many jobs and professions, restrictions were imposed on the education of Jewish children (a "ghetto of desks" was introduced in 1935), and a systematic and severe economic boycott ruined thousands of families. Romania, an ally of France and the West, introduced anti-Semitic legislation around this time. The legislation was passed by the right-wing Romanian government, which nevertheless excluded the Romanian Fascist party, the Iron Guard.

"The Final Solution to the Jewish Problem"

The war brought millions of Jews, quite apart from those of Germany and Austria, under the sway of the Third Reich. By the end of the war over five million Jews, according to the most conservative estimates, had been killed by the Nazis and their allies.

The "final solution to the Jewish problem" is an expression that came into common use in the Nazi bureaucracy in March 1942. It isn't known when the term was coined, because no explicit written order to begin the extermination of the Jews has yet been discovered. But hidden in the bland formula "the final solution" was the objective of the physical elimination, the mass murder, of all European Jews, although the full horror of it would not become apparent until after the war.

One of Hitler's secretaries testified that, even among themselves in private conversation, the Nazi leaders did not speak explicitly of the horrors of the extermination camps. It was almost as if they were aware, more or

Left: two French Jewish women on a street in Paris in 1941. Below: children in a Nazi concentration camp in Carelia (in the USSR near the Finnish border) in 1944.

THE FASCISTS OF SALÒ AND THE JEWS

With the armistice of 18 September 1943, northern and central Italy fell under Nazi control and the politics of the "final solution". From then onwards Jews were hunted down who, up to that point, had been persecuted but lived without threat to their safety. Despite ample assistance from the majority of the Italian people, it has been ascertained that by 1945 one in every six Italian Jews had disappeared into the extermination camps. Half the Jews deported from Italy were arrested between 9 September and 31 December 1943. The biggest deportation was from Rome — home of the largest Jewish community in Italy — on 16 October 1943: 1,259 people were rounded up and 1,023 of them were detained by the Nazis. They were deported to Auschwitz, where eighty-nine per cent of them died in the gas chambers and 167 died during their imprisonment in the camp. Only 1.5 per cent — seventeen individuals — survived.

Liliana Picciotto Fargion has written the most complete study to date of the extermination of Italian Jews (*Il libro della memoria. Gli ebrei deportati dall'Italia, 1943–45*, Milan, Centro di Documentazione ebraica contemporanea, 1991). In it she emphasizes that the Nazi rounding up of Jews was possible because of detailed lists, complete with current addresses. Some of these lists might have been obtained in earlier sequestrations of documents from Roman administrative offices, but most were the result of the bureaucratic diligence of the Fascist state after the anti-Semitic legislation of 1938. Every deportation from Italy was therefore the direct responsibility of the Fascist regime.

While the Nazis hunted down the Jews, the new Republican Fascist state was silent: never has there been a case in which the old Italian saying "He who remains silent consents" was more apt. But it was not enough for the Fascists of Salò to give tacit assent to the deportations carried out by the German occupying army. On 14 November 1943, Police Order 5 was issued, which declared that the Jews "must be sent to special concentration camps" and that "all their goods and property must be sequestered immediately." One of the motives behind this directive was crude and simple: it provided the Nazis with an immediate source of funds.

As to the consequences of Police Order 5, let the figures speak for themselves. In Italy between 9 September 1943 and 25 April 1945 (the day of liberation) 7,013 Jews were arrested. In 4,699 of these cases the agents who made the arrests were noted: Italian agents were responsible for the arrests of 2,210 Jews (of which only 312 were made in collaboration with German agents). It seems likely that the proportion of Italian agents responsible for arrests in this sample is indicative of Italian involvement as a whole. Thus it would appear that the police of Salò — agents of the Mussolini government — were implicated in nearly half of the arrests of Italian Jews.

These figures make it all the more commendable that a great many Italians had the courage and humanity not only to refuse to support the extermination of the Jews but also, and at great personal risk, to help many Jews escape persecution. The attitude of the majority of Italians at the time leaves no doubt that those responsible for the deportation of the Jews from Italy were the Fascists of Salò, who chose to stand by Hitler against the wishes of most of the Italian people. ■

less consciously, of the enormity of what they had set in motion; and they repressed that knowledge in order to defend themselves psychologically. Moreover, it had been necessary to "educate" very intensively those who were to carry out the massacres — to hammer certain ideas into their heads so that they were able to do what they were ordered to do.

In this connection, Reinhard Heydrich's remarks are particularly illuminating. Heydrich was one of the highest officials of the regime's security service; *Reichsprotektor* of Bohemia and Moravia from 1941, he was executed by the Czechoslovakian Resistance on 4 June 1942. A few days before the Nazi offensive against the Soviet Union, Heydrich spoke at a conference of "ideological preparation" for functionaries of the secret police and special units of the Party. He described Judaism to his audience as the greatest danger to the Germans because it was "a hotbed of Communism". To fight effectively against it, it was necessary to extend the scope of extermination operations: these must also include women and children; children above all, in that they were the seeds of future revenge.

Left: Jews arrested by the German SS near Arona in Italy in September 1943. Above: a poster put out by the Nazis in France during the Vichy government. The poster interprets the August 1942 meeting between Churchill and Stalin, in which both agreed to use every means to fight against Nazism, as "the Jewish plot against Europe".

At the end of the war, a high Nazi official explained to the judges of the international Allied tribunal at Nuremburg that the objective was "to reach a state of permanent security, because had we done otherwise these children, whose parents had been killed, would as adults have been no less dangerous than their parents." For this reason hundreds of thousands of children were slaughtered: in the "chaotic eliminations" of the early war years, in the extermination camps, and in mopping-up operations.

From the first, the Nazis maintained that not only among the Jews but also among the "Aryans" there were people who did not deserve to live: the mentally ill, the handicapped, and the carriers of hereditary defects.

The decree that put into practice the long-held principle of the "suppression of lives unworthy of being lived" was issued on 1 September 1939, the day that the Second World War started. "Euthanasia", as they termed the practice of eliminating these "lives unworthy of being lived", was planned scientifically with the enthusiastic support of many famous psychiatrists. The euthanasia campaign contributed two elements to the "final solution" to the Jewish problem: the idea of methodical and organized mass extermination; and the involvement of medical science. In the extermination camps women in particular were used as guinea-pigs, especially in "experimental" methods of sterilization.

"MALE, EIGHTEEN MONTHS, TERRORIST"

In the Apennines near Bologna members of the liberating Allied army read with astonishment an inscription alongside one name in a list of dangerous offenders wanted by the Republican Fascist Guard: "male, two years old, son of a Jewish member of the Resistance, shoot on sight". Another annotation, no less amazing, was found in Drancy, near Paris: "male, eighteen months, terrorist". In the extermination camps, the suitcases of new arrivals were meticulously pierced by bayonet after the guards realized that some of the deportees had hidden babies in them. And pregnant women, carrying new lives within their bodies, were given the same treatment.

What follows is the testimony of an inspector in the SS — that

ruthless military branch of the Nazi Party especially assigned to the "final solution". He describes the act of an SS colonel named Dirlewanger at the time of the so-called

"chaotic eliminations":

"[Dirlewanger] did the following with his young Jewish woman prisoners: he got a group of his close friends together, who were members of a Wehrmacht support unit. They conducted a pseudo-scientific experiment which involved stripping the victims and then injecting them with strychnine. Dirlewanger and his friends observed the scene, smoking cigarettes as these girls died. Immediately afterwards the corpses were cut into pieces, mixed with horse meat, and boiled to make soap."

The inhuman conditions and state of anxiety in which the persecuted Jews were forced to live are given an undying memorial in *The Diary of Anne Frank*, written before she was deported to Bergen-Belsen. ∎

The Efficient Bureaucracy of Death

It was not unusual in the camps for death to come as a liberation, an escape from misery and fear, a regaining of lost dignity. Perhaps the best description of the experience of camp inmates is that of a survivor who now lives in Israel: "The very rhythm of their breathing was of a different nature. We lived and died by laws that were not of this world."

Historians have long discussed, and still discuss today, whether the "final solution" — the systematic destruction of European Jews by means of deportation, death in the gas chambers, death as a result of forced labour, and the most inhuman tortures — was an intentional Nazi project, or rather the consequence of a series of factors that brought Hitler and his men to genocide. Two elements connected with this debate are relevant to the present discussion.

The first, as we have seen, is the potential for violence and destruction inherent in the Nazi anti-Semitic

Top left: a sentry at the Bergen-Belsen extermination camp in front of a truck full of dead bodies. Bottom left: SS Colonel Adolf Eichmann, who played a central role in the extermination of the Jews. He escaped to Argentina in 1945 but was captured by Israeli Secret Service agents, tried, and hanged in Israel in 1962. Below: the writer Primo Levi.

TESTIMONY OF A SURVIVOR: PRIMO LEVI

Stimulated and inculcated for years by state anti-Semitism, hatred of the Jews produces a widespread moral indifference. Primo Levi, an Italian writer and concentration-camp survivor, has thrown light on the subject of the so-called "torturers" of the Nazi concentration camps.

Young people ask us, all the more frequently and insistently as that time recedes into the past, what our "torturers" were like. They use this term to describe our former guards, the SS, and to me it seems inappropriate: it evokes an image of distorted individuals, congenitally warped, sadistic, inherently vicious. But actually they were like us, they were ordinary human beings of average intelligence and average wickedness: with some exceptions, they were not monsters; they had faces like ours, but they had been wrongly educated. They were, for the most part, rough but diligent soldiers and officers: some were fanatically convinced of the Nazi message; many were indifferent, or afraid of punishment, or looking for promotion, or too obedient. All had been subjected to terrible miseducation, supplied and imposed by the schools, at the will of Hitler and his collaborators. ∎
(From: *The Drowned and the Saved* by Primo Levi).

Above: Zyklon B, used in the gas chambers of the Nazi concentration camps. Below: combatants from the revolt of the Warsaw ghetto after they had surrendered. The photograph was taken a few seconds before they were shot.

message. Even if at first the Nazis did not have the *intention* to exterminate, they certainly created the possibility of violently eliminating inferior and dangerous "aliens" from the very inception of their movement. This possibility carried even greater potential for damage because it was "hidden". It should be remembered that modern anti-Semitism is not born of great differences between groups but rather of the threat that those differences will disappear, that Western society will become homogenized, and that the ancient social and legal barriers between Jews and Christians will be abolished.

Raul Hilberg, author of the most important study of the *shoah*, observed that the fate of the European Jews was sealed at the beginning of 1933, when, for the first time, a state functionary used the expression "non-Aryan" in an administrative order. Hilberg's point has a value other than its apparent one of attributing the intention of genocide to the Nazis from the beginning: it suggests that the destruction of the European Jews was perhaps of an even more disturbing character.

H. Feingold's analysis of why the genocide of the Jews is unique in history is illuminating on this point:

The "final solution" was the crossroads at which the European industrial system "strayed from its proper path". Instead of improving the conditions of life, it began to destroy itself. Auschwitz — the largest extermination camp, which has become the symbol of genocide — was also an extension of the modern factory system, where goods were produced but human beings were used as raw materials, and the final product was death. The same comprehensive project was a reflection of the modern scientific spirit having strayed from its proper path. What we witnessed was nothing but an enormous project of social engineering.

It was "social engineering" that could not have been achieved without an efficient modern bureaucracy, staffed by people dedicated to their work and zealous in its performance.

Extermination as the application of modern industrial processes, genocide as the realization of modern bureaucratic methods: in the face of this, it is not enough to say that Nazism and the extermination of the Jews was a return to barbarism, even if, as is obvious, the early phases of the systematic killing of Jews and its occurrence in many regions of Eastern Europe were — even technically — barbaric.

Auschwitz — the largest extermination camp, which has become the symbol of genocide — was also an extension of the modern factory system, where goods were produced, but human beings were used as raw materials, and the final product was death.

Chapter 7

FROM THE **H**OLOCAUST
TO THE **P**RESENT

FIFTY YEARS AFTER THE *SHOAH*, SOME STILL DENY WHAT HAPPENED IN THE NAZI CAMPS, WHILE OTHERS SEE THE HOLOCAUST AS A "NORMAL" PART OF THE VIOLENCE OF THE CENTURY.

In 1945 the "age of the cinema" was already in full swing. The public not only knew what had happened in the extermination camps: they had seen it. Survivors reduced to skeletons, ghosts of their former selves, piles of dead bodies, crematory ovens full of human ashes, heaps of skulls and bones, rooms full of the "by-products" of the industry of death: hair, gold teeth, the frames of pairs of glasses, clothing...

A cremation oven at Dachau extermination camp.
© Publifoto

The shock was enormous. It has been said that it was too much, almost unbearable. Because of this shock, rather than because of the extent of what had happened, the knowledge was repressed, in keeping with a moral attitude already created by the war. With modern military technology, killing had become something distant and impersonal. You press a button; you pull a lever; you study how to raze cities to the ground. The victims are invisible. "Down there on the ground, under the bombardment," writes Eric Hobsbawm, "there were no people about to be burnt or crushed, there were only targets." The same mental mechanism and "ethical justification" presided over the work of many a cog in the machinery of Nazi extermination.

Perhaps, then, rather than speaking of repression it is more precise and useful to speak of stifling shock in a "normality" that accepts and considers as "natural" forms and levels of violence and contempt for human individuals that have long been rejected by the civilized conscience. In this connection, the attitude towards torture is a typical example. As Eduard Peters pointed out in his 1985 book on torture, it came to light after 1945 that at least one-third of the member states of the UN practised torture. And the situation has not improved since then.

Seen from the viewpoint of the use and justification of violence, the twentieth has been a terrifying century, just as it has been an extraordinary century if seen from the viewpoint of technological development. In 1993 Zbigniew Brzezinski — an American political scientist who had been an adviser to President Carter — calculated that during the twentieth century the mass slaughters of war, revolution and racial hatred had claimed 187 million victims. This astounding figure is not simply the direct consequence of the ever-increasing destructive capacity of military hardware: it is rather the result of the effect of that greater destructive capacity on our concepts of war and political strife. War has become "total"; it is no longer, as defined in the *Encyclopaedia Britannica* of 1931, "limited, as far as possible, to posing a threat while not damaging the armed forces of the adversary; otherwise the war would continue to the point at which one of the two sides was exterminated."

THE MINUTES OF THE MEETING AT WANNSEE

On 20 January 1942, a meeting, chaired by Reinhard Heydrich (head of the Security Service of the Reich and SS Obergruppenführer), was held at Wannsee, near Berlin, in which fourteen high officials of the Reich were to "clarify the basic questions" about "the final solution to the Jewish problem". The so-called "Wannsee Protocol" described the future of the Jews in territories under Nazi control.

In the terms of the final solution, the Jews — under proper guidance — will now be assigned to appropriate work activities in the east. In large work teams, subdivided according to sex, Jews who are fit to work will be taken to these territories to build roads, and there is no doubt that many of them will be lost to natural selection. Those who survive, who will without doubt be the strongest, must be dealt with, since they will be the product of natural selection and, if set free, would be the seeds from which a Jewish revival might spring (as history teaches us).

In the course of the practical realization of the final solution, Europe will be sifted from west to east. It will begin with the territories of the Reich, including the protectorates of Bohemia and Moravia, for reasons related to living conditions and sociopolitical order. The evacuated Jews will first be transferred, trainload after trainload, to so-called transition ghettoes, and then transported once again to the east. ∎

(From L. Picciotto Fargion, *Per ignota destinazione. Gli ebrei sotto il nazismo*, Milan, Mondadori, 1994, pp. 217–18).

The shock at the Nazi extermination of the Jews was thus drowned in the "normality" of the violence of the century. This is the foundation of so-called "historical revisionism". There is also a more prosaic and stupid explanation: that which denies the evidence of the facts. According to this reading, the Holocaust simply didn't happen; the genocide of the Jews is, it implies (but only just beneath the surface), a myth created by the Jews themselves in the service of their (imagined) plan for world domination; in short, it is yet another expression of the "Jewish global plot".

The denial of the fact of extermination — a position maintained by self-styled "scholars" such as David Irving in Britain and Robert Faurisson in France — has had a significant following in certain Arab countries and in some Islamic communities. A 1972 article in the journal *Asian and African Studies* contends that from 1956 to 1970 — when Nasser was *rais* of Egypt, the most important and modern of the Arab states — the history textbooks used by Egyptian schoolchildren taught them this version of events. Here is an extract: "In order to awaken compassion, raise money and disguise their expansionist aims, the Jews have always represented the immigrants [into Israel] as persecuted, whereas in fact they have never been... ." This incredible passage is less surprising if we recall Nasser's attitude when, in 1964, he declared to *Deutsche Nationalzeitung*, a right-wing German weekly: "Nobody takes seriously the lie that six million Jews were killed."

Some twenty-five years later, Roger Garaudy — an ex-Marxist, ex-Christian French philosopher — repeated the nonsense that the Holocaust never happened, with "irrefutable" proofs such as the fact that there were survivors. The "alleged" *shoah* is nothing — according to him — but the product of Jewish propaganda in the service of Zionist ambitions.

The discovery of the Nazi horrors certainly made it more difficult — almost impossible — to oppose the idea of a Jewish state, understood not only as a place of refuge for the persecuted but also as a guarantee that the Holocaust could never be repeated.

One often hears of a wave of sympathy for the Jews immediately after the Second World War, caused by

> *The discovery of the Nazi horrors certainly made it more difficult — almost impossible — to oppose the idea of a Jewish State, understood not only as a place of refuge for the persecuted but also as a guarantee that the holocaust could never be repeated.*

"the revelation of Auschwitz". It is true that there was sympathy, but there was also something else indubitably prevalent in political circles. Supporting the foundation of the state of Israel allowed Europeans and Americans to exorcise their guilt while allowing their own exclusionary anti-Semitism to remain unchallenged; the effects and consequences of Israel's foundation were unloaded upon the Palestinians. There was another advantage for the West. Palestine was in a region of the globe whose strategic value was increasing because of its enormous oil reserves. It was thought that this region could be kept under more effective and enduring control by the time-honoured method of "divide and conquer".

The founding of Israel, then, had at least as much to do with power politics and the unacknowledged anti-Semitism of the West as it had to do with sympathy for the Holocaust's victims. But the relationship between Israel and the Holocaust has been complicated and dramatic, from the moment of the first meeting between survivors from the camps and Jewish settlers in Palestine — an encounter fraught with pain and incomprehension.

Arab Anti-Semitism

The Jewish subject of the Egyptian school textbooks during the Nasser years, and that of a French Islamic neophyte such as Garaudy, are identical with the Jewish subject of *The Protocols of the Elders of Zion* (which had a very large circulation in the Near East after the Second World War) and of all European anti-Semitic literature. A Pan-Islamic publication of July 1970 claimed that the Jews had invented anti-Semitism and the extermination of their brothers in order to gain their own political ends; in September 1982 (three years after the Camp David peace accords between Israel and Egypt), a writer in *al-Ahram*

— the most authoritative newspaper in Cairo — claimed that 'for a little money' Jews were willing 'to kill and drink the blood of [their] victims'. Two years later, the Saudi Arabian representative at a UN seminar attributed to the *Talmud* an aphorism that states: "A Jew who does not drink the blood of a non-Jew every year is damned for eternity."

Many leaders of the Palestine Liberation Organization have continued in vain to insist upon a clear

Left: a neo-Nazi gathering at Frankfurt in 1976.
Above: anti-Semitic graffiti in an Italian city in the 1960s.

distinction between Jews and Israelis. In 1970 a Palestinian intellectual, denouncing the use of anti-Semitic literature in the struggle against Israel, asked the following questions: "When will we stop being our own worst enemies? When will we cease to use prejudice in our own just cause, thus depriving it of its humanist dimension?"

The explosion of Arab anti-Semitism — the metamorphosis of the struggle against Zionism and then against Israel from a rejection of political ideas and facts to an anti-Jewish campaign — was a sign of weakness and defeat. It has been completely useless in the fight against Israel. Arab anti-Semitism broke out in all its virulence after the foundation of Israel, gaining further momentum after the crushing defeats of Arab nations in 1956 and 1967, and this is no coincidence. At its root, however, is an older kind of myopia: that of the many Arab nationalist leaders who saw a victory for Germany and the Axis powers as an opportunity to end Anglo-French control of the Near East. Writing of the atmosphere that reigned in Syria in the 1930s, an Arab nationalist leader commented in his memoirs: "We were racists and full of admiration for the Nazis; we devoured their publications and the works that had inspired them."

Even if it didn't help in the fight against Israel, anti-Semitism has served its "classical" purpose in the Near East: it has distracted the people from their actual conditions, directing all their energies instead against an

imaginary earthly Satan and his plots to make Islam suffer.

Another effect of the emergence of an Arab anti-Semitic crusade was that of causing racist fringe groups to emerge in Israel. The idea of the superiority of European and American civilization and its progressive "mission" with regard to colonized peoples has been widespread among Zionists.The germ of racism is there, and, as the Orientalist Bernard Lewis has pointed out, "racism is a contagious evil". Thus we read in the newspapers that, after a massacre of Lebanese civilians in April 1996, Israeli soldiers declared that killing Arab civilians was no great sin.

There is, however, a basic difference between the Israeli situation and those of most Arab and Islamic countries. Every Israeli has access to a vast body of research on the Arabs, their history, culture and religious traditions. By contrast, someone who reads only Arabic may never learn that the authenticity of *The Protocols* has already been disproved. While scientific studies by Israeli scholars have contributed to the world's understanding of Arabic civilization, the dissemination of anti-Semitic literature in the Arab nations and the development of Islamic anti-Semitic literature have worked together to spread anti-Jewish prejudice in places where it was unknown up until a few years ago, such as parts of Africa and southeast Asia.

There is another version of "historical revisionism" that is more popular, subtler, and for many more attractive; its best-known representative is the German Ernst Nolte. According to this reading, the *shoah* — a historical fact and much to be condemned — was the result of a self-defensive reflex against the "Asiatic" barbarisms of the Bolshevik Revolution. Thus, in essence, the violence of the century is used as an excuse — a justification which, being totally generic, is therefore completely lacking in analytical force. Any specific analysis of the Holocaust and its real causes is avoided. It is only apparently paradoxical that the same school of thought has produced a huge literature denouncing barbarism (and the Holocaust, in practice, was certainly barbaric). In both cases the fundamental task is avoided: that of rigorously dissecting the phenomenology of hatred of the Jews and its fullest expression — the Holocaust.

Often silence is the preferred choice, and two Italian examples will serve here. In 1995 Sergio Romano, an authoritative historical commentator, reviewed a book by one of the most important poets of the century — Ezra Pound. Romano did not find it necessary to mention the fact that Pound was an active pro-Nazi propagandist and anti-Semite. In 1996 Einaudi and Gallimard, two highly-prestigious publishing houses, issued a collection of the works of Louis-Ferdinand Céline in their jointly-produced series *La Plèiade*. *L'Unità* — the newspaper founded by Antonio Gramsci and the organ of the most important party of the Italian left — published extracts from Gianni Celati's introduction and a description of Céline in which we are reminded that he was "a controversial author but is considered one of the fathers of the new literature of desperation". Céline wrote pages of anti-Semitic ravings, but for the reader of *L'Unità*, who is not necessarily well-versed in history, this particular detail was not mentioned.

Why this silence? After the Holocaust, anti-Semitism was considered deplorable; certainly no intellectual or artist could both express anti-Semitic ideas and be highly esteemed in the post-war world. The message

Left: the French writer Louis-Ferdinand Céline (1894–1961). Below: Pope John XXIII.

was absolutely clear: anti-Semitism was dross, a tool of reactionary politicians who addressed themselves to reactionary followers.

The truth was otherwise. Many commentators have observed that Shylock in Shakespeare's *The Merchant of Venice* is a typical literary anti-Jewish stereotype. Are the works of Shakespeare a marginal and reactionary expression of European culture? Of course not. As we have seen in the course of this discussion, anti-Semitism can and does co-exist with high culture; modernity (as expressed by such diverse figures as the socialist utopians, Wagner, and Henry Ford) is full of it; it pervades the Christian imagination even in recent times. It was precisely the lack of any great effort to analyze rigorously the culture, popular notions and conditioned mental reflexes of Europeans that permitted anti-Semitism to persist as a disturbing presence in the post-war and post-*shoah* world, no matter how solemnly it is condemned.

How large and how dangerous is that presence? Recently Simon Wiesenthal — who has dedicated his life to documenting the horrors of the extermination camps and encouraging the prosecution of the authors of those inhuman crimes — has reassured those who fear a repetition of the Holocaust: he maintains that the new generations of Germans and Europeans have been vaccinated against that infection.

History does not repeat itself; this much is clear. Nevertheless there are lasting phenomena that resur-

face, perhaps in different forms, like underground rivers. Would it have been possible for anti-Zionism to mask a strong and persistent anti-Semitism if the aforementioned analytical effort had been made on a large scale: the painful but necessary effort to bring European and American culture to self-awareness?

Naturally, it is completely legitimate to think — as many Jewish and non-Jewish critics alike do — that the Zionist solution was a mistake. It is completely illegitimate, on the other hand, to demonize a political project on the basis that it is the expression of the "malevolent nature" of a "race".

If in many ways the picture is sketchy up to this point, significant changes have occurred in the analysis of the Holocaust and its causes, in reflections on anti-Semitism, and in the attitude of the Catholic Church. This last is of particular importance: it is clear, as we have seen, that there is a strong religious substratum even in "modern" and "scientific" anti-Semitic prejudice and hatred. The *Nostra Aetate* (In our time) declaration adopted at the Second Vatican Council on 26 October 1965 was thus an important step towards a future progressive reappraisal of anti-Jewish sentiment. It marked the beginning of a self-critical reassessment of the Catholic Church. In the Council document (which has been denounced by many Arab governments as the product of pressure from "Zionized cardinals") the ancient accusation of Christ-killing was withdrawn in that "even if the Jewish authorities and their followers were instrumental in the death of Christ, what was done during His Passion cannot be even indirectly attributed to all the Jews then living or to the Jews of our time", Jews who share "such a great... spiritual heritage" with Christians. It is no accident that the declaration ends with a chapter on "universal brotherhood, which excludes all discrimination".

However, a rigorous examination of anti-Semitism, its origins and causes, and the desire of many Jews to continue to be "different", requires more than — to quote again from *Nostra Aetate* — the removal of "the foundations of every theory and practice that divides man from man, people from people: discrimination in matters of human dignity and human rights". It requires a different outlook, especially on the real and problematic question of the identity of each person and of different human groups in a world that, becoming ever more global, is at risk of becoming ever more impersonal.

Left: the bench for the accused at the Nuremberg trials.
Above: a survivor of the Bergen-Belsen extermination camp.

Bibliography

■ Z. Bauman, *Modernity and the Holocaust* (Cornell University Press, 1992)

■ H. Berding, *Modern Anti-Semitism in Germany (Moderner Antisemitismus in Deutschland)* (Suhrkamp, Frankfurt am Main, 1988)

■ J. D. Bredin, *The Affair: The Case of Alfred Dreyfus* (G. Braziller Inc., 1987)

■ M. Burns, *Dreyfus: A Family Affair* (Harper, 1992)

■ N. Cohn, *Warrant for Genocide: The Myth of the Jewish World Conspiracy.* (Eyre & Spottiswoode, 1967)

■ R. Finzi, *Marxism, Jewish Worlds, and the Jewish Question* in *Jewishness and Anti-Jewishness: Image and Prejudice (Marxismi, Mondi Ebraici, Judenfrage* in *Ebraismo e Antiebraismo: Immagine e Preguidizio)* (La Giuntina, Florence, 1989)

■ R. Hilberg, *The Destruction of the European Jews* (Holmes & Meier, 1985)

■ R. Hilberg, *Perpetrators, Victims, Bystanders: The Jewish Catastrophe 1933–1945* (Harper Collins, 1993)

■ D. I. Kertzer, *The Kidnapping of Edgardo Mortara* (Vintage, 1998)

■ N. L. Kleeblatt, ed. *The Dreyfus Affair: Art, Truth and Justice* (University of California, 1987)

■ G. Langmuir, *Towards a Definition of Antisemitism* (University of California Press, 1990)

■ P. Levi, *The Drowned and the Saved* (Vintage, 1989)

■ P. Levi, *Moments of Reprieve* (Michael Joseph, 1986)

■ B. Lewis, *Semites and Anti-Semites: An Inquiry Into Conflict and Prejudice* (Norton, 1986)

■ A. S. Lindeman, *The Jew Accused: Three Anti-Semitic Affairs* (Cambridge University Press, 1991)

■ M. R. Marrus, *The Holocaust in History* (Plume, 1989/Bramdeis University Press, 1987)

■ L. Poliakov, *The History of Anti-Semitism* (Routledge & Kegan Paul, 1979)

■ L. Poliakov, *The Aryan Myth* (Basic Books, 1974)

■ J. P. Sartre, *Anti-Semite and Jew* (Schocken Books, 1946)

■ L. B. Steiman, *Paths to Genocide: Anti-Semitism in Western History* (St Martin's Press, 1997)

■ P. A. Taguieff, ed., *The Protocols of the Elders of Zion (Les Protocoles des Sages de Sion)* (Berg International Paris, 1992)

■ E. Traverso, *The Marxists and the Jewish Question* (Humanities Press, 1994)

■ R. S. Wistrich, *Antisemitism: The Longest Hatred* (Pantheon/Methuen, 1991)

■ V. Zaslavsky and R. Brym, *Flight from the Empire* (St Martin's Press, 1983)

■ E. Zola *et al*, *The Dreyfus Affair: J'Accuse and Other Writings* (Yale University Press, 1996)

Index of names

A
Agulhon, Maurice, 12
Alexander the Great, 69
Alexander II, Tsar, 69
Alexander III, Tsar, 47, 54
Alfonso X, of Castile, 15
Arendt, Hannah, 97
Augustus, Caesar, 69

B
Bahr, Hermann, 50
Barnavi, Eli, 103
Bauer, Otto, 81
Bebel, August Friedrich, 79
Benedict XV, Pope, 67, 68

Berding, H., 44
Bismarck, Otto von, 47
Bökel, Otto, 49
Börne, Ludwig, pseudonym of Baruch, Loew, 19
Boulanger, Georges, 36
Bredin, Jean-Denis, 11
Brzezinski, Zbigniew, 118

C
Charles Ferdinand Bourbon, 36
Carnot, Marie François Sadi, 11
Carter, James, 118
Caserio, Sante, 11
Celati, Gianni, 123

Céline, Louis-Ferdinand, 123
Chagall, Marc, 83
Chamberlain, Houston Stewart, 76, 93, 94, 95, 96
Churchill, Winston, 66, 111
Clemenceau, Georges, 33
Costa-Gavras, Constantin, 87
Crémieux, Adolphe, 28

D
Degas, Edgar, 37
de Gobineau, Joseph-Arthur, 20, 93
de Lagarde, Paul, 93, 94
de Lesseps, Ferdinand, 22
de Sepúlveda, Juan Ginés, 8

Deutz, Simon, 36
Dirlewanger, 112
Dreyfus, Alfred, 9, 11, 12, 17, 19, 20, 24, 31, 32, 33, 34, 35, 36, 37, 41, 43, 69, 78
Dreyfus, Mathieu, 32
Drumont, Edouard, 20, 21, 22, 23, 36, 41, 63
du Chayla, Alexandre, 63
Duclert, V., 36
Dühring, Karl Eugen, 93

E
Ehrenburg, Ilya Gregorievich, 86, 87
Eichmann, Adolf, 102, 103, 113
Einstein, Albert, 97, 101
Emeliov, Valery, 85
Esterhazy, Ferdinand, 32, 34

F
Faisal, King, 62
Fargion, Liliana Picciotto, 110, 118
Faure, François Felix, 33
Faurisson, Robert, 119
Ferrer, Vincenzo, 14
Feingold, H.,114
Ford, Henry, 74, 75, 76, 124
Förster, Bernard, 52
Fourier, Charles, 20
Franz Josef, 26
Freud, Sigmund, 101

G
Garaudy, Roger, 119, 120
Gasparri, Pietro, 68
Gemelli, Father Agostino, 98
Genghis Khan, 9
Goebbels, P. Joseph, 97, 100, 101
Gohier, Urban, 61
Goldmann, Nahum, 84
Gramsci, Antonio, 123
Greive, H., 50
Grynszpan, Herschel, 102
Gromyko, Andrei, 84
Grossman, Vasili, 86

H
Hart, Solomon Alexander, 47
Heine, Heinrich, 97
Hemardinger, 36
Henry, Duke of Chambord, 36
Henry, Emile, 11
Henry, Hubert-Joseph, 31, 34
Heydrich, Reinhard, 103, 111, 118
Herzl, Theodor, 37, 38, 39
Hilberg, Raul, 103, 114
Hilton, John, 72
Hindenberg, Paul Ludwig, 89, 102

Hitler, Adolf, 47, 48, 68, 74, 75, 76, 87, 89, 90, 91, 93, 95, 96, 97, 99, 100, 101, 102, 109, 110, 113
Hobsbawm, Eric, 117

I
Irving, David, 119

J
Jesus Christ, 23, 25
Jobert, Michel, 62
John XXIII, Pope, 123
Joly, Maurice, 64
Jouin, Ernest, 68
Judas Iscariot, 13, 25

K
Kaganovich, Lazar Moiseevich, 85
Kaufmann, Isidore, 51
Kautsky, Karl, 81
Kublai Khan, 9

L
Laval, Pierre, 107
Lazare, Bernard, 33
Lenin, Vladimir Ilyich, 67, 77, 79, 82
Levi, Primo, 113
Lewis, Bernard, 122
Litvinov, M. Maksimovich, 84, 85
London, Arthur, 87
Lueger, Karl, 46, 47
Louis Philippe, d'Orléans, 36

M
Maimonides, Moses, 18
Mayer, Simon, 36
Maria Caroline Duchess of Berry, 36
Marr, Wilhelm, 43, 47
Marx, Karl, 15, 20, 51, 97
Mehmet, Ali, Viceroy of Egypt, 28
Meyer, Arthur, 36
Meyer, Naquet, 36
Mercier, Auguste, 32
Momigliano, Felice, 98
Mommsen, Theodor, 50, 51
Montand, Yves, 87
Montefiore, Moses, 27, 28
Moro, Aldo, 63
Mortara, Edgardo, 9, 26
Mussolini, Benito, 108, 110

N
Napoleon Bonaparte, 69
Napoleon III, 26, 64, 69
Nasser, G. Abd el, 62, 119, 120
Neher-Bernheim, R., 69
Nicolas II, Tsar, 63
Nietzsche, Friedrich, 52-53
Nilus, S. Alexsandrovich, 62, 64
Nolte, Ernst, 122
Nuwaihid, Ajjai, 69

P
Parker, Alan, 76
Pétain, Philippe, 106, 107
Peters, E., 117
Picquart, Georges, 32, 34
Pius IX, pope, 26
Poliakov, Léon, 14, 36, 76
Polo, Marco, 9
Pound, Ezra, 123
Preziosi, Giovanni, 61, 64, 68
Proudhon, Pierre-Joseph, 20
Proust, Marcel, 20

Q
Qaddafi, Muammar, 63

R
Ramazzini, Bernardino, 13
Renoir, Auguste, 37
Retcliffe, John, 65
Ritter, 46
Romano, Sergio, 123
Roosevelt, Theodore, 93
Rosenberg, Alfred, 90, 91, 93, 96
Rosenberg, Ethel and Julius, 87
Rosenfelder, Fritz, 98
Rothschild, banking family, 18, 22, 25
Rothschild, Nathaniel, 25

S
Sartre, Jean-Paul, 79
Schiff, 73
Shakespeare, William, 124
Shaw, George Bernard, 64, 93
Sombart, Werner, 51
Stalin, J. V. Djugashvili, 78, 79, 83, 84, 85, 87, 111
Stöcker, Adolf, 47, 48
Strauss, Levi, 71, 73
Streicher, Julius, 100
Sutton, A., 67

T
Tanguieff, P. A., 69
Taxil, Léo, 63
Tolstoy, Leo, 93
Toussenel, Alphonse, 20, 24
Treitschke, Heinrich von, 50, 51
Trotsky, Leon, 69, 73, 77, 84

U
Urban II, Pope, 14

W
Wagner, Richard, 49, 50, 51, 76, 93, 124
Wiesenthal, Simon, 124
Willrich, Wolfgang, 95

Z
Zola, Emile, 33, 34, 35

The Traveller's History Series